THE BIBLE CODE: FACT OR FAKE?

The Bible Code
Fact or Fake?

PHIL STANTON

KINGSWAY PUBLICATIONS
EASTBOURNE

ISBN 0 85476 766 5

Designed and produced by Bookprint Creative Services
P.O. Box 827, BN21 3YJ, England, for
KINGSWAY PUBLICATIONS
Lottbridge Drove, Eastbourne, East Sussex BN23 6NT.
Printed in Great Britain.

*Thank you, Beatriz,
for your invaluable help
in the preparation of this book.*

Contents

Introduction

Why Read On?

When *The Bible Code*[1] first came out, it created considerable interest and not just among believers. People started talking about it, and Christians are being asked what they think.

But the issue is much wider than that. The Bible itself is at stake. As we shall see, there is far more to all of this than first appears. Why has the Bible Code become bestselling news? Is it really a sign that people may be returning to the true God, or is it a move even further away?

I set out to answer these questions in the pages that follow.

Although this book was written primarily for Christians, it was not so exclusively. Folk *are* talking about these 'sensational new discoveries', and the Bible is on many people's lips in a new way. Christians need to be able to say what they think, and how it affects the essential issues of life. But, beyond that, the Bible Code raises questions that are of the highest importance; questions Christians cannot afford to ignore.

What, for instance, do we believe about the Bible? Do we believe it is God's book? If so, do we know *why* we believe that? And if it is God's book, why is it so little

---

[1]Michael Drosnin, *The Bible Code* (Weidenfeld & Nicolson, 1997).

known? Does the Bible Code itself give us a clue in this vital matter?

Yes, the Bible Code raises more issues than might at first appear. It goes beyond merely the sensational, the exciting. It forces us to decide what we believe, and why – and whether we are living consistently with those beliefs.

So we start with the Bible Code, and then move on to weightier matters – matters that none of us can afford to ignore.

1
The Truth Is Out There

'Spectacular revelations!'
'Amazing discoveries – is this the end of the world?'
'Secrets lost since the dawn of history!'

What do these phrases provoke in you? Be honest, what is your natural reaction? Some of us are sceptical about anything like this. 'It's a load of old rubbish,' we say before we have even read the book. Others of us rather like the idea that vital truths have been hidden; we read the book, and then tell all our friends about it.

I suppose I am a bit of both. I *do* believe that we are kept in the dark about some things – things that are really important – but I don't like the sensationalism for its own sake.

The Bible Code[1] is certainly sensational, and it claims to bring vital revelations to light. Does it? Is it fact or fake? I intend to show that when we examine the evidence, we find that the Bible Code is fake.

But it is not a pointless fake. We have much to learn from it. Examining the Bible Code will be like an excavation. We shall dig further and further down, uncovering deeper and deeper levels. Once we have

---

[1]Michael Drosnin, *The Bible Code* (Weidenfeld & Nicolson, 1997). All quotations are from the hardback version.

reached the heart of the matter, we shall build from there. We shall see what the real secret is.

There are amazing revelations in *The Bible Code*. I believe that we shall find a cover-up that affects all of us in a vital manner. We are being misled, although not intentionally so far as Michael Drosnin is concerned. The issues at stake are enormous. *The Bible Code* is part of the deception, but it is far bigger than just this one book.

I ask the reader to accompany me, as I go through the evidence and make the logical conclusions. I shall be drawing considerably from the Bible, and I shall be giving those who don't believe it some pretty strong reasons why they should.

When I said that the issue is much bigger than just *The Bible Code*, what did I mean?

Atlantis, UFOs and the conspiracy theory

We are, they tell us, in the scientific age. We don't believe things merely because we are told to. We want proof; we want to sift the evidence. Why is it, then, that we are not satisfied with what the orthodox scientists tell us? Why does it sometimes seem so dull and uneventful? Because we don't find their views engrossing. That is why there has been such a flood of unorthodox revelations over the last few years. Ancient records have been plundered for mysteries. Plato said something about an island that sank, called Atlantis. From this tiny seed, endless books have arisen, feeding the curiosity many feel. Was this island *really* in the area of the Bermuda Triangle, and is that *really* the accident spot some claim it to be?

Most people prefer to stay in the dark about Jesus Christ; so why is there such interest in the cup he used at the Last Supper? The Holy Grail appeared in the old accounts of King Arthur, as a Christian motif. Now it is an ancient mystery. Does it contain the secret of youth? It did when Indiana Jones found it.

Another fascination is with UFOs. Are there really such things? There seems to be *something*, certainly, but is it an influx of benign aliens, eager to woo us to the ways of peace? That is how they appear on many popular television series, and the special effects are so good that we feel we have actually seen them! But are we really interested in the facts? Most UFO enthusiasts seem unaware of powerful evidence that would unseat their theories.

Not that they think they *are* theories – they survive on a carefully controlled diet of information that confirms their view. It is taken for granted that there has been a cover-up by the American government; that the authorities are suppressing vital evidence about UFOs. This is called 'the conspiracy theory', and it takes many different forms. Some people find it easy to believe in a conspiracy theory. The amazing revelation that they have had (whatever it is) must, they feel, be known to the authorities. Why is it suppressed? There must be a sinister motive. Another view of the conspiracy theory is that a small group of powerful people are deceiving us for their evil ends. There are as many forms of the conspiracy theory as there are paranoid people.

Suppressed evidence

But, of course, there is nothing new about the idea that powerful people will try to manipulate the masses. Hitler used propaganda to keep the German people under his rule. By the time his deceptions had been laid bare, the country was in ruins.

The fact is, it is in the interests of some people that the masses never hear certain embarrassing truths. And remember, *we* are the masses! What is being kept from us?

Amid the sensational and unbalanced books, might there not be some lone witnesses to the truth?

Many years ago, for instance, I read a book called *Secrets of the Lost Races*.[1] You couldn't have a much more sensational title than that, and it was written by a journalist, like many of the wildest of these books are. Yet when I read it I found that it contained fascinating records of discoveries that related to life before Noah's great flood. These included machine-worked objects found in the coal strata. So why sensationalise the data? Because orthodox scientists believe in evolution. They believe that the coal strata must have been formed millions of years before mankind. They simply cannot afford to permit us to know about these things. Belief in evolution is fundamental to modern society.

Another book that revealed information embarrassing for evolutionism was *The Facts of Life*,[2] again by a journalist. All he did was to pass on some of the data that is well known to scientists but kept from ordinary people. Such data cannot fail to discredit the theory of evolution.

Another unorthodox writer was Immanuel Velikovsky. His amazing *Ages in Chaos*[3] came out in 1952, and was virtually banned by the establishment. Why would anyone want to ban a book about the chronology of ancient Egypt? The answer is that Velikovsky corrected the errors of the orthodox – and the experts did not like it. Worse still, his new chronology confirmed the Bible.

What do these examples have in common? In each case, suppressed evidence has been revealed to challenge our society's rejection of the Bible. Since the system doesn't permit the data to be released in the normal way, the writers

---

[1] Rene Noorbergen, *Secrets of the Lost Races* (New English Library, 1977).
[2] Richard Milton, *The Facts of Life* (Fourth Estate, 1992).
[3] My copy published by Abacus in 1973.

have had to descend to sensationalism in order to get into print at all.

But isn't this what *The Bible Code* does? Is it not reaffirming the Bible in a sensational fashion? It seems to, but it doesn't, as we shall see. In fact *The Bible Code* is part of the suppression of the Bible.

The suppression of the Bible

The reader may wonder whether I am being a little paranoid. After all, aren't Bibles available everywhere? Don't they have them in school? If the Bible were suppressed, wouldn't it be unavailable?

The thing is, it used to be unavailable, but that policy didn't work. The authorities have been forced to find another approach. We see forcible suppression of the Bible in the days of the Roman Empire. They burned Bibles, and the people who owned them. Nothing should have been impossible to pagan Rome. After all, what power did the Christians have? They lacked power and money, and refused to use force.

Yet, in spite of all their advantages, pagan Rome lost. Out of the ashes of the old empire a new Roman Empire arose, based on the Bible. This was the thousand-year empire of Byzantium. In Europe the Bible was honoured, but it was banned once more by the time of the Reformation (sixteenth century). Once again it meant death to have a Bible written in your own language. Many heroes – Bible translators, printers and preachers – had to die before the battle was won. The Bible triumphed and became the basis of society in reformed countries.

So the lesson of history is this: governments that ban the Bible will fall.

But Western society is determined to live without the Bible. The underlying policies of government are mostly anti-biblical. Those in power know that they would lose their power if the Bible were accepted by the people. How could they be rid of this irrepressible book?

Since force could not work, they used propaganda. Schools, universities, television – even some theologians – have projected a false idea of the Bible. It all amounts to this: the Bible, they say, can be disproved or, at least, it cannot be proved. They pronounce that it isn't solid fact, and it does not transform lives. None of these things is true, but people are so indoctrinated that they do not check the facts.

The truth is in here

In today's tangle of propaganda and popular belief, it is clarity we need. There is a revelation to be had, and it is sensational beyond the wildest dreams of the most avid sensation-hunter! There is no need to take my word for it: the essential facts are available to anyone, as we shall see.

But before we open that door, we are going to look at *The Bible Code*, which has attracted so much attention of late. The reader will learn some vital facts not mentioned in that bestseller. This will set the so-called Bible Code in a completely different light.

But we shall not stop there. We shall trace the deception to its root, which goes far deeper than this current sensational bestseller. Michael Drosnin can say that, so far as he is aware, 'I have no preconceived beliefs' and 'nothing is taken on faith' (pp. 11–12), but is this really so? We shall find that, beneath the apparent objectivity of today's Westerner, there is a very definite belief, and a great deal is taken on faith.

Far from being ruled by a true scientific objectivity, today's attitude to the Bible is irrational and escapist.

But this is entirely unnecessary. We shall follow the facts

wherever they lead, and find that the Bible has a 'code' very different from what many expect. We shall find the one truly sensational fact, and examine the extraordinary implications for us.

So, are we ready? We shall try to put prejudices and preconceived notions aside and start with *The Bible Code*, the beginning of our trail.

2
Ancient Wisdom?

What is the Bible Code? To put it simply, it is finding
words amid a great mass of letters – rather like the word
puzzles that some people enjoy. The letters come from the
Old Testament. Finding words is so complex that extremely
powerful computers are used.

However, despite the complexity, the basic idea is simple
enough. We could even try it ourselves. For instance, if we
took the words I have already written in this chapter, and
arranged them in a series of rows, the result would look like
this:

W	H	A	T	I	S	T	H	E	B	I	B	L	E	C	O	D	E	T	O	P	U	T	I
T	S	I	M	P	L	Y	I	T	I	S	F	I	N	D	I	N	G	W	O	R	D	S	A
M	I	D	A	G	R	E	A	T	M	A	S	S	O	F	L	E	T	T	E	R	S	R	A
T	H	E	R	L	I	K	E	T	H	E	W	O	R	D	P	U	Z	Z	L	E	S	T	H
A	T	S	O	M	E	P	E	O	P	L	E	E	N	J	O	Y	T	H	E	L	E	T	T
E	R	S	C	O	M	E	F	R	O	M	T	H	E	O	L	D	T	E	S	T	A	M	E
N	T	F	I	N	D	I	N	G	W	O	R	D	S	I	S	S	O	C	O	M	P	L	E
X	T	H	A	T	E	X	T	R	E	M	E	L	Y	P	O	W	E	R	F	U	L	C	O
M	P	U	T	E	R	S	A	R	E	U	S	E	D										

Can you find any words in this? You can look for them
vertically, horizontally, or even diagonally. You can read
them backwards if you like. If you shorten the lines, you
find the pattern changes:

W	H	A	T	I	S	T	H	E	B	I	B	L	E	C	O	D	E
T	O	P	U	T	I	T	S	I	M	P	L	Y	I	T	I	S	F
I	N	D	I	N	G	W	O	R	D	S	A	M	I	D	A	G	R
E	A	T	M	A	S	S	O	F	L	E	T	T	E	R	S	R	A
T	H	E	R	L	I	K	E	T	H	E	W	O	R	D	P	U	Z
Z	L	E	S	T	H	A	T	S	O	M	E	P	E	O	P	L	E
E	N	J	O	Y	T	H	E	L	E	T	T	E	R	S	C	O	M
E	F	R	O	M	T	H	E	O	L	D	T	E	S	T	A	M	E
N	T	F	I	N	D	I	N	G	W	O	R	D	S	I	S	S	O
C	O	M	P	L	E	X	T	H	A	T	E	X	T	R	E	M	E
L	Y	P	O	W	E	R	F	U	L	C	O	M	P	U	T	E	R
S	A	R	E	U	S	E	D										

Now you can start all over again! There is a whole new range of possibilities to find horizontal and vertical sequences.

With lines of any length in the Bible Code, there is an almost infinite number of different arrangements of the letters! So don't think you could try this on your home computer!

In the Bible Code, the computer expert looks for specific words, such as 'Hitler', and if he finds them, he looks for other words nearby that fit with Hitler, such as 'Nazi' or 'concentration camp'. If such words are found together, it is taken as a prediction that Hitler would arise, establish a Nazi party and set up concentration camps. Several such 'amazing predictions' are found in the Bible Code but, alas, there is a trick, as we shall see in the next chapter.

But even if we are overawed by the wonders of modern technology, we need not switch off our common sense. Let us think a little about this.

Wisdom or foolishness?

It is claimed that the Bible Code predicts 'everything … all that was, is, and will be' (p. 44). This is an amazing claim, that the Code is entirely correct *and* covers the whole of life.

Just think what it means: these miraculous predictions cannot be accidental. Who, then, has encoded these predictions into the ancient text? It cannot be any mere human: it must be God. That would mean that God inspired the Old Testament.

But here comes the dreadful contradiction. Michael Drosnin says: 'I'm not religious. I don't even believe in God. I'm a total sceptic' (p. 181). In other words, he doesn't give any weight to the words of the Old Testament. If he did, he would believe in God.

Imagine yourself to be this champion of the Bible Code. When you examine the actual letters of the Old Testament, looking for coded predictions, you are amazed at the accuracy and foreknowledge of the Bible. But then if you actually *read* the Bible, you are entirely unimpressed! On the one hand the Bible is all-knowing and wise. On the other it is unworthy of the least belief. Surely this is a massive contradiction!

Remember that the Bible Code works from the text of the Old Testament. Surely you can't have it both ways. If these letters are highly significant in the Bible Code, surely the same letters cannot be ignored in the Bible! The 'Someone' who arranged these letters so exactly did so originally in the form of teaching. The tiniest detail of the letters is all-important in the Bible Code, yet the actual meaning of these letters, in the words they originally formed, is meaningless! Does that make any sense at all?

Who put the code there? Michael Drosnin says: 'I'm not religious. I don't even believe in God.' No human could have done it, since no one knows the future – not, at least, in this complete way. It requires more-than-natural (ie supernatural) power. So to whom does Mr Drosnin turn?

Spacemen to the rescue

Alas, he turns to spacemen. Those who are familiar with books of the sensationalist genre know that alien spacemen are a popular way to explain away the supernatural. The great pioneer in this respect was Erich Von Daniken, whose *Chariots of the Gods*,[1] and numerous sequels, established the fashion.

Von Daniken's work has long since been discredited, but spacemen remain a useful refuge for the sensationalist. The idea is that alien spacemen with superhuman powers visited earth regularly in the past. What they said and did was entirely misunderstood by everybody, so these spacemen accidentally started all the mutually contradictory religions. Sadly, they left no definite evidence of their visits, and they have not returned. Of course, some say that they have returned, hence encounters with UFOs in our day. But here again the facts are on the other side. A survey of the UFO data shows that these sightings and encounters (where they have no natural explanation) are more likely to be occult.[2] These spacemen have no basis in fact. They are simply a useful cop-out: they are sufficiently supernatural to explain miracles, without being God and thus commanding our obedience.

This is what Michael Drosnin says: 'The Bible Code is, in fact ... "an alien artefact"' (p. 98). These aliens were supernatural enough to know the future perfectly, but they were also human enough that we have no need to think about God.

This reminds us of the beliefs of ancient paganism. They had their gods, who were a mixture of supernatural power

---

[1] Erich Von Daniken, *Chariots of the Gods* (Bantam Books, 1971).
[2] See John Keel, *UFOs – Operation Trojan Horse* (Abacus, 1973) and Eric Inglesby, *UFOs and the Christian* (Regency Press, 1978).

and all-too-human weaknesses. These gods lived on some high mountain, such as Mount Olympus. They were far enough away to be unlike the true God who fills all things, and yet powerful enough to take the place of God in people's minds. Instead of living up in some far-off galaxy, these gods lived up in some far-off mountain.

No doubt these 'gods', when they appeared, were as demonic as the 'UFO-nauts' who appear to naive enthusiasts today.

The more you think about it, the more ridiculous it seems. Mr Drosnin remarks, casually, that 'three thousand years ago, the Bible was encoded' (p. 28), but actually, the Old Testament was not written at one time. About a thousand years elapsed between the time of Moses and the time of Malachi, the last prophet. Think what this would have meant to these aliens!

Remember, the Bible Code depends on *every letter* in the Old Testament being accurately written down. To do this, the aliens would have had to make sure each writer wrote the words down exactly. What an enormous job that would have been! They could not have allowed the slightest error, and they would have had to do it again and again over a thousand years without the people they used to pen the Old Testament guessing who they were really working for!

If that were not ridiculous enough, these aliens would have had to oversee the copying of the Old Testament right up to the invention of printing. After all, errors can easily creep in when you copy massive books by hand. And again, the copiers must never realise that they were interacting with aliens!

We have powerful reasons, as we shall see, to believe that the Bible has been preserved over the centuries. But only God could do it.

A proof of God?

It would be tempting to subscribe to the Bible Code theory
and use it as proof of God and the Bible. This seems to
have been done by some of the Jewish experts whom
Drosnin quotes. But I suggest that this is a temptation
Christians must resist. For one thing, there is already ample
proof of God and the Bible (more about this in Chapter 5),
so we don't need to use dubious proofs. For another, the
Bible Code seems to give a wrong idea of God.

Look at the contrast between the true God of the Bible,
and the 'god' of the Bible Code.

The true God speaks openly. 'I have not spoken in
secret,' he says, 'in a dark place of the earth' (Isaiah 45:19).
Moses and the prophets proclaimed what became the Old
Testament. They preached it, and tried to get everyone to
listen. Moses' law was read publicly on a regular basis
(Deuteronomy 31:10–13).

There is no 'secret tradition' in the Bible. All that
belongs to the cults. But the Bible Code is a secret
revelation, something that has been hidden for thousands of
years. It simply isn't the style of the true God.

What's more, God is looking for humility in his listeners:
'On this one will I look: on him who is poor and of a
contrite spirit, and who trembles at My word' (Isaiah 66:2).
But the message of the Bible Code is only available to
those who can afford the most powerful computers, and
have the intellectual gifts to use them.

In other words, the Bible is for the poor and humble, and
the Bible Code is for the rich and clever.

The contrasts go further. The message of the Bible is
about Christ and salvation. The prophets called for
repentance and faith. There are amazing predictions in the
Old Testament, which were remarkably fulfilled in the
earthly life of Christ. But God never shows any interest in

predictions *for their own sake*.

The Bible Code is in complete contrast to that. The Bible Code does nothing to encourage repentance and faith, as we can see from the example of Michael Drosnin. Although he is an enthusiastic supporter of the Bible Code, he 'could not believe in supernatural salvation' (p. 91). The Bible Code gives predictions for their own sake. There is no reason given, no view of life – just the predictions.

The central fact about the true God is that he is absolutely sovereign. Jesus, the Son of God, says, 'All authority has been given to Me in heaven and on earth' (Matthew 28:18). No one who believes the Bible could dare to rival God in his authority and power.

It is all very different with the Bible Code. For one thing, it seems that 'all probabilities are in the Bible Code' (p. 44). In other words, it is suggested that the predictions in it can be averted. So they are not absolute predictions. What does this mean? 'Maybe it was done this way to preserve free will' is the answer.

In the Bible, threatened punishments can be averted, but only by repentance and faith (see Jeremiah 18:8; Jonah 3:4–10). It is very different in the Bible Code. The disasters can be averted without any thought of repentance and faith – without, in fact, any reference to God at all. *The Bible Code* gives exciting narrative of the author struggling to save the world from a nuclear holocaust.

The key authority is not God at all, but human free will. In other words, humanity – not God – is the authority. 'If the Bible Code came from an all-powerful God, he would not need to tell us the future. He could change it himself' (p. 103). No, an all-powerful God would not fit with the message and style of the Bible Code. That is why I think Christians should be very cautious about using the Bible Code idea in their witness to the world. I think it is regrettable that Grant Jeffrey uses the Bible Code so confidently. His book *The Signature of God* gives some excellent reasons to believe the Bible to be God's book. He has no need to bring in the Bible Code, or to affirm that the Bible Code material 'is possibly the most important evidence that I shall present in this book that will prove to any unprejudiced observer that the Scriptures are truly inspired by God'.[1]

A little over the top?

It may seem highly impressive that not only all futures, but 'all probabilities are in the Bible Code' (p. 44), but surely this goes beyond the most outrageous claims of the most confident fortune-tellers. The more we think about it, however, the less impressive this sounds because what it means is that the Bible Code predicts nothing. If all probabilities are there, how can we tell which one is going to happen? 'All probabilities may be there, and what we do may determine what happens' (p. 44). We can determine which of the possible futures will happen. But if we can do this by deliberate actions, so too, presumably, we can do it by mistake.

Let us think about what this means. Suppose you had lived in the 1930s and had access to the Bible Code. Suppose for a minute that the Bible genuinely predicts Hitler's life (we shall see in the next chapter that it doesn't). You see Hitler rising to power. You discover, from the Bible Code, that he will cause great damage. Perhaps you deliberately run him over in your car. Hitler never becomes the famous monster that he became. No one ever bothers to look for his name in the Bible Code, and no one knows what nearly happened.

---

[1]Grant Jeffrey, *The Signature of God* (Frontier Research Publications Inc, 1996), p. 202.

All this makes for a good science fiction story, but we are dealing with real life here. Of course no one had the Bible Code in the 1930s, but there were plenty of bad drivers then as now. Why couldn't someone have run Hitler over by accident? If the horrors of the 1940s could have been avoided had the Bible Code been known, then they could have been avoided by accident.

In fact, an ancestor of Hitler, many centuries ago, could have been killed accidentally. This could have meant that Hitler was never born. Perhaps someone completely different could have been given the name Adolf Hitler – someone good, who would have been a wonderful leader for Germany. So how do you know that the 'Adolf Hitler' who is rising to power will be the Nazi tyrant? It could be a nice Hitler, because a vital ancestor had been accidentally killed long before.

If all this is sounding more and more complicated, don't blame me! The Bible Code predicts everything – and nothing. We wonder why the alien spacemen bothered to put it in the Bible in the first place...

All this is in dramatic contrast with the Bible.

A number of specific predictions are given in the Bible. These refer to Christ, to the church and to whole nations. Some still await fulfilment, but many have come true, literally and unmistakably. Nobody, deliberately or otherwise, has managed to change the future that the Bible predicts.

To take one of thousands of examples, we read that the imperial city of Babylon 'will never be inhabited, nor will it be settled from generation to generation' (Isaiah 13:20). Most ancient seats of empire, such as Rome and Byzantium, remain inhabited. But Babylon is in ruins. The fulfilment came many centuries after Isaiah's time, and was not brought about by Bible-believers.

A powerful ruler tried recently to rebuild Babylon. His

name was Saddam Hussein,[1] and traumatic events forced
him to abandon the project...

What about Rabin?

Much of *The Bible Code* narrates – as only a journalist can
– the story of how Mr Drosnin tried to save President
Rabin's life. Yitzhak Rabin was assassinated in 1995.
Unlike the other Bible Code predictions, this one came
before the event. In fact, Mr Drosnin tried to warn Rabin,
and was, not surprisingly, ignored.

But Rabin *did* die. How do I explain that?

There are a number of possible explanations. I believe Mr
Drosnin's story – his book bears all the marks of sincerity –
but it is not impossible that his memory may have been at
fault in places, or that others involved may have viewed
matters differently. Mr Drosnin is not infallible so far as his
memory is concerned, any more than the rest of us are.

For instance, Mr Drosnin recalls a conversation with
Rabbi Steinsaltz, an international expert on the Hebrew
language. This is how he reports it: '"In the Bible time is
reversed," said Steinsaltz, noting an odd quirk in the
original Hebrew text of the Old Testament. "The future is
always written in the past tense, and the past is always
written in the future tense"' (p. 175).

Clearly Mr Drosnin is reporting the conversation as
accurately as he is able, and I'm sure his memory is better
than mine, but one thing is sure: Rabbi Steinsaltz did *not*
say this. This isn't true of Hebrew. If it were, then the tense
'always written' for the past would be called 'the past
tense', not the 'future'.[2] I can guess what Rabbi Steinsaltz
said, because I know a little Hebrew. I can understand all

---

[1]George Grant, *Blood on the Moon* (Wolgemuth & Hyatt, 1991), p. 29.
[2]See the Appendix on the Hebrew language for a fuller discussion.

too well how Mr Drosnin could have misheard or misunderstood him.

There is something else that Mr Drosnin may not be aware of. The Hebrew base their calendar on the years of the world (AM = Anno Mundi). The year that Mr Rabin died was 1995 (5756 AM), and this was the year that was found in the Bible Code. But was 1995 really 5756 years from the creation of the world? Mr Drosnin, who appears to be an evolutionist, would certainly say 'no'. But what is the view of those who accept the Bible? Surely the spacemen would expect us to use the system of chronology that appears in their Bible.

And it is here that the complications arise. The Bible gives a reasonably clear chronology, but it is impossible to arrive at complete certainty of the exact dates. According to the classic evangelical chronology the creation was dated at 4004 BC. This would make AD 1995 to be 5999 AM, several years away from the date given in the Bible Code for Rabin's death.

Other Bible-based scholars give dates that vary by several decades. The uncertainty doesn't affect anything of importance from the point of view of the Bible, but it makes all the difference to the Bible Code. On the classic dating, 5756 AM, when Rabin was to die, would be 243 years ago. Did it refer to another Yitzhak Rabin? Was it one of the probable futures that never happened?

After all, why should the Jewish dating be the correct one from the point of view of the spacemen? Mr Drosnin makes it clear that although the Bible Code is in Hebrew, 'the information is for everyone' (p. 20). So why shouldn't the classic Christian dating, based as it is on the same Hebrew Old Testament, be rejected? In fact, since absolute certainty is missing when it comes to the age of the world, how can we interpret these dates at all?

In any case, I would suggest a very different explanation for Mr Drosnin's foreknowledge of Rabin's death.

Unseen, but not inactive

History records many occult predictions, many of which were proved false, but there have been a few which have come true. Usually, these have been predictions of disasters. This is still the case: most prognostications we hear of (outside the church) are warnings of dire events. 'Beware the ides of March!' Julius Caesar was warned – and sure enough, he died at that time. Mr Drosnin's prediction of Rabin's death fits the general pattern: it *was* a disaster; it *did* come true. And, also fitting with the general pattern, Mr Drosnin's other predictions in the Bible Code, concerning nuclear war and attacks on Israel, have *not* come true.

His explanation is that he has averted the disasters (so far). This is how I see it: only God knows the future.

> Let all the nations be gathered together,
> And let the people be assembled.
> Who among them can declare this,
> And show us former things?
> Let them bring out their witnesses,
>   that they may be justified;
> Or let them hear and say, 'It is truth.'
> 'You are My witnesses,' says the LORD,
> 'And My servant whom I have chosen,
> That you may know and believe Me,
> And understand that I am He.
> Before Me there was no God formed,
> Nor shall there be after Me.'
>   (Isaiah 43:9–10)

The Bible teaches us that any supernatural predictions which are not from God must be from the devil. How then can the devil predict future things, as he so often has done, through false prophets, clairvoyants and the rest? Although he doesn't *know* what will happen, he knows what evil people are planning. Of course he knows – he is involved in cooking up many of those very plans! No doubt he was deeply involved with President Rabin's assassin.

This seems to me to explain the phenomenon. This is why the predictions are usually about disasters – these are things that the devil knows about in advance. That is why the predictions don't come true very often – the devil is only guessing. He doesn't really *know* the future.

Mr Drosnin has no belief in the supernatural – either in God or the devil. He would not knowingly follow the devil, but sadly the supernatural doesn't go away just because you don't believe in it. The God that Mr Drosnin doesn't accept *does* rule the universe. The devil that Mr Drosnin does not mention in the book still 'works in the sons of disobedience' (Ephesians 2:2).

It would be no hard task (for the devil) to suggest to someone like Mr Drosnin that he search for Mr Rabin's name using the Bible Code, and then look for words meaning 'assassin', 'murderer', 'killer' and so on, nearby it. Since the devil knew that Mr Rabin's assassination was being planned, this presents no problem. When the devil suggests ideas to people in real life, there are no claps of thunder, no shadowy figures. You just feel that an idea has come into your mind. That suits the devil fine. He is not looking for publicity.

I hope no one misunderstands what I have said. The apostle John says: 'We know that we are of God, and the whole world lies under the sway of the wicked one' (1 John 5:19). So this is no particular reproach on the purveyors of the Bible Code; I am not suggesting that they are any more 'under the sway of the wicked one' than anyone else. In fact, one cannot help admiring Mr Drosnin's wholehearted attempts to save the world from imminent catastrophe.

But however good a person's intentions, the devil is at work. And his work is trickery and deception.

Spot the queen

There is a card trick that proves highly successful in relieving the naive of their money. You are shown three cards, one of which is the queen. They are then shuffled face down, and you have to follow the queen with your eyes. If you succeed, you win the money. You think you have kept track of the queen, but when you make your guess, you find you are wrong. You haven't merely lost face, you have lost your cash. It's all a trick.

Something very similar is happening here. We thought *The Bible Code* was a sensational book about events predicted in advance with amazing accuracy. We find that it predicts nothing with certainty. In fact, you need to know what you are looking for before you look – no one would search for 'Hitler' unless they already knew that he would be a major figure. And since the future is notoriously unpredictable, the Bible Code (even if it gave reliable predictions) would be of little help.

Meanwhile, no one is bothering to read the Bible. There are so many clear predictions in the Bible with fulfilments in history. Here is the real sensation! Why skip over it in pursuit of something far less sure and certain?

When Mr Drosnin does quote biblical prophecy, he shows that he is no expert on the Bible. Why should he be? He is no believer, and no doubt his journalistic research keeps him pretty busy. I merely mention it lest someone, skimming through *The Bible Code,* sees mention of the book of Revelation and thinks that biblical prophecy is being seriously studied.

All Bible Code, no Bible. I think we are being tricked.

Rather than reveal the future, the Bible Code takes our eyes off the real revelation. Instead of reading the Bible, with its amazing track record of fulfilled prophecies and more to come, people ignore it. They just feed it into their

computer and get a bewildering mish-mash of futures –
possible, probable and actual.

Is someone trying to keep us in the dark about what is
really in the future? Is there a conspiracy of silence? Are
we supposed to take our eyes off the Bible, because
something far more sensational is here?

'Conspiracy!' someone says. 'The man is paranoid!'
Well, what explanation would *you* give? The Bible, which
used to be familiar to everyone in the West, has gradually
fallen into neglect. Even Christians are often found to be
woefully ignorant of its contents. Why?

No one has actually proved any error in the Bible; all its
predictions so far have come true; wherever it is known and
believed, wonderful transformations occur in ordinary folk.
So, why ignore it?

The Bible is as remarkable as it always was, and more so
since advances in science and knowledge have failed to
uncover a single mistake in it. It is almost as if some secret
force has duped us. We thought we could spot the queen;
now we wonder how the trick was done. We've been had.

The further we go in this investigation, the more we shall
understand the forces in society around us, and the more we
shall learn to 'spot the queen'.

3

It's All Hebrew to Me

It seems utterly amazing that famous names such as 'Adolf Hitler' should be present in the Bible Code. Mr Drosnin tells us that a similar search in *War and Peace* – like the Old Testament, a large book – produced no such names. Does this not prove that there is some sort of code in the Bible?

No.

When they put the Old Testament into the computer, they left out the vowels and the spaces between the letters. This destroys the meanings of words in any language, and especially in Hebrew.

Think what it would mean in English. Consider the word 'hello'. If the vowels were removed, it would be unpronounceable: 'HLL'. If you tried to say this, it would convey nothing at all, and if you wrote it down, it would be anyone's guess what you meant; maybe 'hell'.

Things are even worse when you leave out the spaces between the letters. 'Hello, Simon' becomes 'HLLSMN' which might mean 'Hell is mine' or 'Hills man'. 'PHLPSTNTN' ('Philip Stanton') could mean 'Philip is too neat? – no!'.

Of course there are times when the meaning would still be obvious: 'XT' on a door has to be 'exit'. Again, 'KNGRTHR' on an ancient monument would probably be

'King Arthur'. The reason we could guess some of these words is that they are what we expect to find. This is certainly not true of the Old Testament. If you have read it, you will know this. It is an amazing revelation, quite unlike anything you might expect.

If vowels are essential for English, they are far more so for Hebrew. For example, the English word 'word' would be 'WRD' with the vowel removed. 'WRD' could be:

Wired
Weird
Ward

Any reader able to double this list should award himself a prize!

The Hebrew for 'word' is *'dabar'*. When you take the vowels out you get 'DBR', which can be any of the following:

Speaking
To speak
He spoke
Debir (the name of a town)
The word of
Speak!
Pasture
Plague
He destroyed

All these actually appear in the Old Testament.[1] Obviously, having the right vowels makes a great deal of difference. A sheep, for instance, would like to know it is getting

---

[1] See B. Davidson, *The Analytical Hebrew and Chaldee Lexicon* (Bagster & Sons, no date).

'pasture', not merely a 'word' (you can't eat words), or even the 'plague'!

And all this is without running several words together! Because the vowels make more difference in Hebrew than they do in English, there is a greater range of misunderstanding in Hebrew without the vowels than there would be in English.

So, using a vowel-less Old Testament in the Bible Code guarantees that it will say anything. Mr Drosnin puts in whatever vowels he needs to make 'the Bible' say what he wants. To illustrate this, I tried a little experiment of my own.

My own code

I have my own book *Samson: The Secret of Strength*[1] still on my computer. I took the final chapter, and removed the vowels and spaces between the words. I then used a typeface that makes every letter the same width, so that I could read the letters vertically and diagonally, as well as horizontally.

I then did a Michael Drosnin, and looked up my name: 'PHLP' (which doesn't appear in the original chapter). I lengthened and shortened the lines, so that I could find the right letters in the right places. Once I found my name, I looked around the same area to see what other words I could find.

This is what I got:

---

[1] Published by Kingsway, 1996.

M	Y	S	K	W	L	L	F	N	D	T	M	T	T	H	W	N	T	D	T	H	N	T	H
S	N	S	F	C	S	N	G	T	X	S	T	D	T	D	T	H	T	M	R	N	N	N	G
M	Y	L	F	F	N	C	S	S	R	Y	W	W	L	L	G	V	R	L	V	S	F	R	C
H	R	S	T	S	S	K	F	C	L	L	D	W	S	H	L	L	D	M	G	H	T	V	X
P	L	T	S	F	R	J	S	S	W	R	O	L	L	Y	W	L	L	N	G	T	S	F	F
R	F	R	H	M	F	R	T	Y	T	H	S	D	N	G	R	N	T	D	N	D	H	L	F
F	C	H	R	S	T	N	T	N	L	Y	T	D	L	V	N	H	M	D	T	L	S	T	S
F	F	R	F	R	H	S	S	K	P	H	L	P	P	N	S	S	S	T	H	D	L	L	S	N
R	C	R	T	D	W	R	L	L	Y	W	N	T	T	H	S	C	R	T	F	S	T	R	N
G	T	H	P	R	W	R	D	Y	T	L	Y	D	W	N	R	W	N	D	S	R	S	P	L

Above the 'PHLP' there was a 'STNTN' – 'PHiLiP
STaNToN'. How amazing! No doubt *War and Peace* could
not yield such an extraordinary combination; unless, of
course, its vowels too were left out.

Encouraged by this, I set out to see what might be
predicted of me in this remarkable code. Should I, for
instance, be writing this present book? What could I learn
of my future?

As I looked at the letters, suddenly all became clear to me.
The letters 'THRYS' appeared, in a diagonal arrangement.
Clearly this meant 'auTHoR? – YeS!'. What a remarkable
prediction! I hastened to fulfil it.

I trust that Mr Drosnin will forgive this ironic imitation
of *The Bible Code* approach. And, just in case some readers
plan to take this a bit further, please don't. I know that
'FLR' – obviously 'FaiLuRe' – is there, and I don't want to
hear any other bad news! Mind you, I'm sure that 'failure'
is only a probable future, and will never happen!

All humour aside, it is clear that you can get almost
anything you want if you feed consonants into a computer.
This would work just as well with *War and Peace*, or any
other book, as long as the vowels were missing. And we
have seen that the vowels are even more important in the
Hebrew language, since without them words have so many
different meanings.

The Bible Code is not amazing at all. It would work with any book, provided one left out the vowels and ran the words together. So, how have they got away with it? To understand this, we need to know a little about the Hebrew language.

The Hebrew language

Most of us have seen Hebrew writing – perhaps in television pictures from Israel, or written on the outside of a synagogue. The Hebrew letters look so strange that we never expect to understand anything at all. But Hebrew is not that complicated. After all, tiny Hebrew children learn it.

Hebrew is written back-to-front. Most of the letters are very different from ours, but not all. The Hebrew 'c' sound looks very much like our 'C', but back-to-front. The biggest difference is that in Hebrew the letters are the consonants: B, C, D, F, etc. What about the vowels? The Hebrew vowel sounds are written in a system of dots (called 'points'). So my name, Philip Stanton, in the Hebrew style would be something like this: PH.L.P; ST:NT'N – except that the dots should be in, on or under the consonants.

As well as vowel points, there is a punctuation dot in each word. This separates the words, even if they are written without spaces. So, the vowels and the spaces are conveyed by points (dots). These are very fiddly to write, and the possibilities of making a tiny (but highly significant) mistake are very great. Also, the vowels can only be seen when you look closely, whereas the consonants can be read from a distance.

Because of this, inscriptions were written without vowel points. The dots would be difficult to see, and they would disappear with erosion anyway. And then a little seed might be blown on to the inscription, and look like a vowel point!

In the days when books were copied by hand, producing a full Hebrew Old Testament (with dots) would be a massive project. Of course, this was sometimes done, but not always. It would be much cheaper to have one without any dots at all. If you were reasonably familiar with the Old Testament, you would probably remember what the vowels were, and you would save the enormous cost of a full version.

As soon as printing was invented, the Hebrew Old Testament was printed in its full ('pointed') form, copied from the many handwritten manuscripts. Nowadays, when you buy a Hebrew Old Testament, it has all the vowels and punctuation. (You can see what it is like from the cover of this book.) But it takes ages to write Hebrew vowels and punctuation marks, and it is hard not to make one or two mistakes. The vowel and punctuation points are so sophisticated that you would need too many keys for a typewriter. I have three Hebrew typefaces on my computer, but none has the full system of points, or anywhere close. (See the Appendix for more about the Hebrew language.)

There are two theories on how the vowels have been preserved. The classic view is that they were written from the beginning, by Moses and the prophets. The modern view is that they were remembered faithfully, and then written in much later. In ancient times, people had a far greater ability to remember information than we have today.

I prefer the classic view. It fits better with what Jesus said about 'every jot and tittle', as we shall see. Hebrew students who are not familiar with it should read John Owen (seventeenth century), who wrote a powerful book on the subject.[1] In it he established the traditional view that the vowels in our Hebrew Bibles were written from the

---

[1] 'Integrity and Purity of the Hebrew and Greek Text', in *The Works of John Owen* (reprinted by the Banner of Truth Trust, 1968), vol. 16, pp. 345–424.

very beginning. He answered the arguments that the vowels
were added later.

Another writer, the scholar-pastor John Gill, traces the
vowels back to Old Testament times, through references in
ancient records.[1]

Either way the case is clear: the Old Testament without
vowels (whether in Hebrew or English) is meaningless.

He never told us...

But it is this meaningless 'Old Testament' that the Bible
Code uses! Mr Drosnin acknowledges that the spaces
between words are left out. He quotes a 'legend' (!) that
'Moses received the Bible from God ... without break of
words' (p. 25). But he doesn't mention that such breaks
would be supplied by the punctuation dots anyway.

What does he say about the missing vowels? Nothing at
all! This is nothing short of amazing. The Bible is mutilated
before being used for the Bible Code, and we are not told.
If I did not know Hebrew, perhaps I would have been
convinced by Mr Drosnin's book.

Those who *are* convinced are going to feel cheated. They
were never told the simplest of facts. They were deceived
(possibly by accident) into thinking that the real Bible was
used in the Bible Code.

This explains why the New Testament is not used. Mr
Drosnin has no prejudice against the New Testament; he
gives his view of biblical prophecy, and refers to the book
of Revelation. The reason the New Testament is not used in
the Bible Code is that in Greek (the language of the New
Testament) the vowels are much like English vowels. They
are conveyed by letters, just like the consonants. If these

---

[1]'A Dissertation Concerning the Antiquity of the Hebrew Language', in
The Works of John Gill (my copy dated 1778).

were left out (as they would have to be for the Bible Code to work), it would be too obvious; the trick would be exposed.

The amazing dates in the Bible Code are also easily explained. What Mr Drosnin doesn't tell us is that, in Hebrew, the letters were used as numbers. This was usually the case in ancient languages. We see this in Roman numerals – for instance, 1997 = MCMXCVII. These letters are also used to make up words, but where they stand for numbers, it is obvious. This is why we read, in Revelation 13:18, that 'the number of the beast is 666'. In the Greek this is not '6 – 6 – 6' but 'six hundred and sixty-six'. This means that if you add up the numerical value of the letters of the beast's name, it would come to the total of 666. Similarly, if you add up the numerical value of the Greek letters for 'Jesus', you get 888.

So there is nothing impressive about finding dates in the Bible Code. All the consonants have a numerical value, so there are as many dates as you could ask for.

Smokescreen

The whole Bible Code falls apart when we realise that the vowels are missing. But don't think that you've spotted all the tricks yet. The scholars behind the Bible Code know Hebrew perfectly well. They know the vowels are missing. They knew it was best not to tell us about it.

But why? Why did they bother with this Bible Code?

Whether they know it or not, the Bible Code is part of a giant cover-up, and we need to get to the bottom of it. I trust we shall get to the heart of the matter in Chapter 5, but meanwhile let's look at the clues before us.

The Bible Code *seems* to affirm the Bible. But the Bible it uses is mere gibberish; unpronounceable without the vowels. You could change the translation in almost every

verse until its meaning suited you. The Bible Code seems
sensational while the Bible seems fruitless. In other words,
the Bible Code is really attacking the Bible while
apparently supporting it. We see this in an exchange
between Mr Drosnin and Eli Rips, who is trying to
convince him about the Code. Mr Drosnin writes: 'I picked
up a Bible from the desk in his study, and asked Rips to
show me the Gulf War. Instead of opening the Bible, he
turned on his computer. "The Bible Code is a computer
program," he explained' (p. 19).

Do we see the significance of this? Don't bother to pick
up the Bible! It's not in the words of the Bible that the truth
lies, but in its vowel-less gibberish. The fact is, 'the real
message of the Bible Code is just the opposite' from that of
the Bible (p. 103).

This becomes clearer when we see what Mr Drosnin says
about the real Bible. He tells us that he believes there to be
no God, so we would not expect him to read the Bible for
his own benefit. But he makes use of biblical prophecy to
build up an idea of an impending 'Armageddon'. As a
journalist, he must be experienced in painstaking research
and reading endless documents.

So when we see how he interprets the Bible, we realise
that he has little respect for it. Had he a real respect for the
Bible, surely he would have approached it with more
humility and thoughtfulness. He would have studied the
insights of those who have become mighty in the
Scriptures. As it is, he makes some amazingly unhappy
attempts at interpreting the Bible.

Here are some examples. Mr Drosnin is only really
interested in finding apocalyptic pictures in the Bible:
'[Daniel and Revelation] are predictions of unprecedented
horror' (p. 85). Anyone who actually reads these biblical
books will find a lot more than mere 'horror'. There is
glory, praise and joy. Surely Mr Drosnin isn't saying that

the thought of Christians in heaven is one of 'unprecedented horror'?

'The early Christians believed that the New Testament clearly stated that the end would come in their own lifetimes. Did not Christ warn "This generation shall not pass away till all these things have happened"?' (p. 94). The 'end' that Mr Drosnin intends is a cataclysmic end of the world. Christians did *not* believe that this would happen in their own lifetimes – they didn't know when it would happen (and still don't). Jesus' words (Matthew 24:34) referred to another 'end': the destruction of Jerusalem and its temple, which happened in AD 70. Christians saw shadows of events still in the future in Matthew 24, but its direct reference was to 'the buildings of the temple. And Jesus said to them, "Do you not see all these things? Assuredly, I say to you, not one stone shall be left here upon another, that shall not be thrown down"' (Matthew 24:1–2).

Anyway, this is what the early Christians thought. If Mr Drosnin had consulted, for instance, 'The Church History of Eusebius' (born around AD 260), he would have seen that the Christians in Jerusalem escaped its siege and destruction because they 'had been commanded by a revelation … to leave the city'. The siege that followed is described by Eusebius in terms of Matthew 24, even to the 'abomination of desolation'.[1]

A little research would have shown Mr Drosnin that he had misread the New Testament passage. But rather than carry out the research, it was easier for him to write that Jesus was wrong in his predictions.

There is neither space nor necessity to list all of Mr Drosnin's weaknesses in understanding the Bible. One

---

[1]'The Church History of Eusebius', in *The Nicene and Post-Nicene Fathers*, Second Series, Vol. 1, p. 138, Bk 3, Chp. 5.

more example will suffice: '"To see the future you must look backwards," states the Book of Isaiah' (p. 105). Anyone even moderately familiar with the Bible knows that no such sentiment appears in Isaiah, or any other part of the Bible. 'To see the future, you must look up [to God]' might express an aspect of the Bible message.

Let me make it clear that I am not making any sort of personal attack on Mr Drosnin. After all, he makes no claim to be interested in the Bible – only the Bible Code ('There is a Bible beneath the Bible' [p. 25]). I quote these mistakes to point to an underlying theme.

The Bible Code is part of the war against the Bible.

Faint praise

There is an old saying that people are 'damned by faint praise'. It means that you can humiliate someone better with a tiny compliment than with an outright insult. The reason is because an insult shows that you are against the person, so people don't take what you say too seriously. 'He's biased,' they think. But if you offer a minimal compliment, it can be more humiliating. 'You can see he wanted to say something nice,' people say, 'but there just wasn't much he could say.'

When this book is reviewed, someone might write: 'Complete rubbish, a total waste of time; use it to start your garden bonfire.' If this is written, I shall just assume that the writer does not like my position. I might even feel complimented: they are angry because they can't rebut my arguments. But if someone says: 'A noble effort, sincerely carried out, with humour as its strongest point. Sadly a little weak in its use of arguments,' then I shall go away and cry.

The old pagans said, 'Burn the Bible, and the people who read it.' This didn't work. The Bible Code says: 'The Bible is amazing, but don't bother to read it.' Their apparent support for the Bible, their praise for its predictive powers, seems to put them on the 'right' side. So when *they* make it clear that the Bible is not worth reading, it is all the more convincing.

This leads me to another question: Why are they doing it? I don't mean merely the originators of the Bible Code, but the whole system. After all, the Bible Code has been publicised, promoted and made a bestseller.

What happens when someone writes a book showing the real wonders of the Bible? Does the system promote it? Is it publicised? Can it reach the bestseller list?

The answer, of course, is no.

There is no shortage of really good books about the Bible and its riches. Many of these are virtually unknown, even in church circles, to our shame.

So what is going on? Books that oppose the Bible, books that damn it with faint praise – these get the publicity and exposure. Books that offer something really marvellous are consigned to silence.

And remember, the books I refer to are honest: they face up to the criticisms of the Bible, and offer rational explanations for people's difficulties. The Bible Code, on the other hand, is plausible *because* it doesn't mention the one essential fact that the vowels are left out.

Are we easily led?

Do you get the impression that 'they' are trying to control the way we think? Is our reading material being censored? Is the system trying to mould us according to a pattern that suits them?

Are we going to let it happen?

What is it that they are so afraid we shall find out? It seems that they can't make society forget entirely about Jesus Christ, so we get the heavily promoted 'Christianity disproved' books. No one ever hears about the Christian books that counter such bestsellers.

But presumably it isn't possible to make people think that there is nothing supernatural in Christianity. And so we get the Bible Code, and its kind, which finds something amazing in the Bible, and then discourages us from reading it. This is how an inoculation works: you are injected with a little of the dangerous disease so that you become immune to it.

The Bible Code inoculates us against the Bible.

That leads us to another question: Why do they fear us reading the Bible? What is in it? Is it like the Bible Code, impressive but ultimately a fake? Or is there solid proof for the factuality of its teachings?

We shall look more at these questions in Chapter 5. Meanwhile, let us be clear on this: the people in power have a lot to lose if we all start following the Bible way. There is more in the Bible than loving one's neighbour. The rich and powerful would not like the 'restrictions' that the Bible puts on unrestrained greed and selfishness.

After all, however powerful you are, you still need to win elections or sell your product. What if people ceased to vote for unprincipled plutocrats? What if they boycotted the products of evil and oppressive companies? What if they judged all the advertising and propaganda by the clear standards of the Bible?

What if they stopped believing what they are told?

Unlikely, you say, but these things have happened. When the God of the Bible begins to transform people, everything changes. It may be that those at the top have been studying a little history. They know how gladly people embrace the teaching of the Bible when they get to hear of it. They know what happens next. They are determined that it isn't going to happen.

Most of us are obedient pawns, responding to all their

propaganda and advertising. We wouldn't dream of having an idea that they haven't approved. You can even see this in the churches.

Do we really know the Bible in the church?

Are we worth persecuting, or are we sufficiently in tune with the system?

4
The New Hierarchy

The Middle Ages are often portrayed as dark ages, in which members of the populace were compelled to believe whatever the priests told them. 'No wonder the people were so stifled,' we hear. 'They weren't allowed the freedom to think.'

However true, or otherwise, that is of the Middle Ages, the implication is that it is *not* true now. Of course, few pay any attention to the ministers of Jesus Christ, but is there a new 'priesthood'? There certainly seems to be, judging by *The Bible Code*.

Aware that his claims are going to sound preposterous, Mr Drosnin is quick to introduce a range of 'scientists', and their confident pronouncements. This puts the ball in our court. Are we going to bow to 'expert' opinion? If we don't, then who do we think we are? Do we think we know as much as the experts?

But if we believe what the scientists tell us, then we might as well stop thinking and let them tell us what to believe. However, it is never *the* scientists, but simply *some* scientists. Many scientists are convinced Christians – their books are among those that the system ignores.

Since the system can choose which scientists to promote, it is the system – not 'science' – which will mould us. There are two kinds of scientist that Mr Drosnin quotes in favour of the Bible Code. There are famous scientists (Newton, Einstein, Hawking), who contribute a general worldview. And then there are the computer experts and code-breakers, who have run the Bible Code through their computers and can verify the results.

A typical saying of the computer expert is: 'The Bible Code is an established fact' (p. 44). The famous scientists declare that there are (have been? will be?) many alternative futures.

How are we going to respond to all this?

Keep your heart

There is a proverb in the Bible which says: 'Keep your heart with all diligence, for out of it spring the issues of life' (Proverbs 4:23). In the Bible the heart symbolises our understanding and decisions. So the proverb means: 'Don't let anyone do your thinking for you!' It is wisdom to learn from others, but we must not surrender our minds to them. The fact that a scientist says something doesn't mean we have to believe it.

Another thing to ask is: 'Is this his area of expertise?' The views of a musician are important when it comes to music, but why should a musician know more than I do about football?

With that in mind, let us listen to the experts whom Mr Drosnin quotes.

Harold Gans, for instance, is 'a senior code-breaker at the top secret National Security Agency' (p. 23). In addition, he speaks Hebrew. He was initially sceptical about the Bible Code, but went on to spend 440 hours checking the Bible Code on computer. His verdict? 'I set out to disprove the code, and ended up proving it' (p. 23).

Other experts are quoted with similar confidence. What are we to say to that?

I ask, '*What* has he proved?' I have no doubt that you can find anything you want to in a vowel-less Old Testament if your lines can be of any length. In fact, in my own humble way I have proved it myself: I found what I wanted in a vowel-less chapter of one my own books (in Chapter 3).

So, impressive as it sounds, this 'proof' from the code-breaker proves nothing. Or rather, all it proves is that the originators of the Bible Code made no mistakes – at least not on the computer. But we never doubted that anyway.

What about the famous scientists?

The technocracy

Albert Einstein and Stephen Hawking are certainly mighty names. Their authority lies in their science. What is 'science'? Science is supposed to be the study of data and the deduction of conclusions (or at least theories) from it. A scientist examines the immense array of data on, for instance, the body of a murdered man, and gives the police vital clues. He will know the time of death, and details of how he died. *We* could never draw the same conclusions, because we don't know how to access or assess the data.

However, if the scientist remarks that the murdered man 'deserved all he got', then he is no longer speaking as a scientist. What blood sample or temperature reading tells him what the man deserved? He is abusing the respect he has as a scientist in order to promote his views as a human being.

So what support do these scientists give for the Bible Code? The answer is: none at all. Or at least nothing scientific. For instance, 'most scientists believe that the Uncertainty Principle is a fundamental, inescapable property of the world' (p. 42). Notice the all-important word 'believe'. This is not science at all, but a belief system. This Uncertainty Principle 'states that there is not one future, but many possible futures' (p. 42). Of course, on one level this is obvious. It may or may not rain next week. There are at least two possible futures, and I cannot tell which is the true one.

But our whole context is the Bible Code, which supposedly predicts future events. Obviously if the future is successfully predicted, as it often is in the Bible, we want to know *how*. The Bible tells us that God knows the future; *the* future – there is only one.

The Bible Code does not predict the future. 'There is a code in the Bible, but we don't know if it is always predictive' (p. 78). 'When the Bible code becomes widely known, and people try to use it to predict the future, they should know that it's complicated. All probabilities may be there, and what we do may determine what actually happens. Maybe it was done this way to preserve free will.'[1]

The Uncertainty Principle is vital at this point. If we accept that there is one future, and that only God can predict it, then we are left with the Bible as the only infallibly accurate book of predictions. But if we say that there are many possible futures, then the indeterminate predictions of the Bible Code are vindicated.

The ordinary person is impressed with an infallible prediction of the future. He is less excited with uncertain predictions that probably won't come true. So to stop him thinking about it, the mighty names of scientists are brought forth.

But is the Uncertainty Principle a scientific matter? After all, where are the data, the tangible discoveries, that point to many possible futures? Have these possible futures left marks by which their existence can be known? Obviously not, because they are still future.

---

[1]Eliyahu Rips in *The Bible Code,* p. 44.

What it boils down to is this: many people believe in man as the nearest thing to God in existence (more about this in the next chapter). If they were right, then everything that man cannot be certain about would *be* uncertain. This could be said by the stamp collector as much as by the scientist. It is no more 'science' than it is philately. If we respected stamp collectors as we do scientists, no doubt *The Bible Code* would refer to them too.

Humble, but not gullible

I am not suggesting that each of us becomes a know-it-all. We need one another. We need each other's insights, gifts and expertise. I just refuse to be enslaved to other people's beliefs.

There is a real danger that we be swept along by the system, but we must resist. Let us look at it this way: the study of the point and purpose of life is called metaphysics – the *why* not just the *how* of existence. In the ancient world, there was real confidence that human thought could give the answer to life. As the various avenues were found to be dead ends, the confidence waned.

Christianity gave ancient philosophy its death blow. The church analysed pagan philosophy with merciless logic. Once Augustine had issued *The City of God* (fifth century), paganism had so many holes visible, it just wouldn't float any more.

The ancient world turned to the Bible, and a new kind of philosophy began. This led, in due course, to the birth of modern science. Many of the first scientists were simply acting out the implications of their biblical faith.[1] This seems largely to have been forgotten. For instance, Eliyahu

---

[1]Henry Morris, *The Biblical Basis of Modern Science* (Baker Book House, 1984), pp. 25-132.

Rips talks as if the Bible and science are in conflict: 'I think that, finally, when we understand both well enough, religion and science will come together' (p. 31). There is, however, no conflict between real Christianity and real science.

In the seventeenth and eighteenth centuries philosophy returned to its old pagan basis. It tried to make sense of life without the Bible. To start with it was full of confidence, as the pagans had been. But gradually philosophy began to hit the same dead ends. Modern philosophy refuses to return to the Bible. It keeps trying. As a result, philosophy has become rather dull. Hardly anyone, except students who have to, seems to read it nowadays. This has led to disastrous consequences. G. K. Chesterton says somewhere that modern philosophies have this in common: they all begin with something monstrously illogical. After that they proceed rationally enough. By 'illogical', Chesterton meant 'against common sense'.

We see this perfectly illustrated in the Bible Code. It is illogical to take the vowels out of a language and then be surprised when all sorts of words can be made out of the lines of consonants. But we are not even told that this is what has been done.

Common sense was sacrificed, but no one came to the funeral. They hadn't been told it was dead.

After this initial irrationality, the Bible Code proceeds logically enough.

Instead of a 'new hierarchy' holding sway over our minds, I appeal to you to hold on to your freedom. Common sense is not to be despised just because it is common to everyone. The obvious logic by which we live our ordinary lives should not be disdained. After all, we use it to drive cars, eat food and conduct our business. Why should it not apply to things like the Bible Code as well?

Common sense

The scientists also live their normal lives by common sense. What do I mean by 'common sense'? As soon as we are born we begin to develop a system of logic based on observation of real life. It is a matter of experimentation and is thus entirely scientific. For instance, if a child puts a bar of chocolate into his pocket, he will get no more than one bar out again. You can't get out more than you put in. He finds the same happens with exams. If he doesn't work to put knowledge into his mind, he won't have it for the exam. Observation tells him that things are really there – something that some modern philosophers choose to doubt. The house he sees is the same one everyone else sees. Unless something disastrous happens, the same house is always there, looking the same.

This is why, in Chapter 2, we looked at the inconsistencies in the idea of the Bible Code. These inconsistencies are offences against common sense.

What do you do when someone comes to your door to sell you something? If you have no common sense, and never acquire any, you will be regularly cheated and burgled. Common sense tells us not to trust strangers until we see evidence of their trustworthiness. We learn that people have motives to do us harm.

If we apply this lesson to someone who may cheat us of our money, it is common sense to apply it to other cheats. We have more to lose than just money. There are those who want to abuse our bodies, dominate our minds and destroy our souls. We have to be on our guard. Common sense tells us that some attacks are physical, but not all. We learn to be wary of subterfuge. Frankly, we are very naive if we swallow the latest idea without guarding ourselves with common sense.

This applies on every level. Suppose, for instance, that

you were walking in a wood and you found a calculator lying on the ground. Imagine there were no markings on it, but you found that it worked. There is one thing that common sense would tell you: someone made this calculator. This would be obvious, whether you understood calculators or not. You would never think that the calculator had come into being by accident. If your friend said that he thought the calculator had simply formed itself naturally, without anyone being involved, what would you say? You would think your friend was joking – or completely mad. He would have departed entirely from common sense.

But this is what many do today. Complex as a calculator is, it doesn't compare with the universe. Whether you look on the large or the small scale, the complexity and genius of it all is mind-boggling. Common sense tells us that this complex and brilliant design must have a designer. The belief that the universe came about by accident, or impersonal evolution, without God is nonsensical.

But that is what is assumed (never scientifically proved) at the very outset. After that things proceed logically enough. But the damage has been done.

We are being invited to surrender common sense, and to trust what some experts tell us.

The miraculous chip

Another 'expert' to whom we are called to submit is the computer. The last few years have seen a complete revolution in how we live, brought on by the marvellous computer. Everything is run with the help of computers.

Some older people find it hard to adjust their thinking to the computer age; young people have never known anything different. Things that seemed impossible a few years ago are perfectly easy now.

They used to say, 'The camera never lies.' If it is there

on film, it must be real. Nowadays, a photograph is easily adjusted on a simple computer program. Life-like dinosaurs can be seen stalking the modern world in (apparently) complete realism, computer-generated in the latest movies.

At the end of the day, however, the computer is just a machine. All it does is make mathematical calculations, but it does them so fast that all these marvels become easy.

The disciple of evolutionism is looking for the next step in evolution, and expecting mankind to make it happen. To them, it seems that a computer only needs an advanced 'artificial intelligence' (ie, a soul), and then it will be superior to man.

Those who think like that have forgotten that the computer is no more than an extremely sophisticated adding machine. The whole idea is beautifully parodied in *Life, the Universe and Everything*.[1] In the story, an amazingly sophisticated computer is built, the size of a planet. Once built, this ultimate computer, called Deep Thought, is asked the answer to the vital question of life, the universe and everything.

Deep Thought, of course, has not only a human-like soul, but a fine selection of human-like behaviour problems as well. Once asked, he (it?) begins to work out the answer, while religious leaders of all persuasions wait in painful anticipation.

At long last the computer returns the answer. The answer to the question of life, the universe and everything is 42! After all, what would you expect from an adding machine?!

The power of computers

People put so much store in the computer. It is as if

---

[1] The third of the *Hitchhiker's Guide to the Universe* by Douglas Adams (William Heinemann Ltd, 1982).

computers have a greater-than-human ability to think things through. If something has been 'proved' by a computer, then who are we, mere humans, to challenge it? Computers are definitely part of the new hierarchy.

In reality, computers never do anything except what they are asked to – and sometimes not even that. If you were to ask a computer whether there is a God, you would have to tell it what you think the evidence is, what weight it should give to different kinds of data, and so on. If you were looking for the answer 'no', it would not be hard to make sure you got it.

In the Bible Code, the computer simply looks for configurations of letters. It doesn't know that the Hebrew vowels are left out, because it only knows what it is told. It has never looked at a real Hebrew Old Testament. It doesn't know that there is a cover-up going on, and it wouldn't care even if it did. It is not going to heaven or hell – only the scrapyard. It neither knows nor cares about our eternal destiny.

In fact, so far as the real issues of the Bible Code are concerned, the computer is quite incapable of having anything useful to say at all!

The Bible Code seems to rest upon the powerful impression made by the mere word 'computer'. It is a mistake to be impressed. Once we understand what computers have done to establish the Bible Code, we see that they never address the real issues at all.

We must resist the prestige of the computer.

Christians and the Bible Code

Christians put a lot of weight on what they hear from Christian leaders. It is obviously too early to get an assessment from the church, but what about *Yeshua*?[1] This

---

[1] Yacov Ramsbel, *Yeshua* (Frontier Research Publications, 1996).

book was written by a Christian eager to use the Bible Code
to bring Jews to Christ.

Mr Ramsbel displays great love and concern for his
fellow-Jews, and he tries to promote their best interests. He
deserves their gratitude, and everyone's admiration. The
whole style of his book makes it clear that he loves God so
much that he wants to please him above everything else.

But although I look up to Mr Ramsbel as a Christian, I
cannot agree with his approach. I think he should have
stayed with the classic and irrefutable proofs of Christ in
the Old Testament. The danger is that once the Bible Code
is fully exploded, Mr Ramsbel's appeal to Jews will be set
aside as well.

His book goes through the Old Testament and finds
Jesus' name and vital gospel words 'encoded' everywhere.
We have seen that you can find anything from a massive
selection of consonants. The interesting thing about his
book is that it prints the Hebrew with its essential vowel
points and, sometimes, punctuation marks. He even gives
the reader helpful tips about the language. It just doesn't
seem to have struck him that the Bible Code is based on the
absence of vowels and punctuation.

This book uses the Bible Code idea, but doesn't justify or
explain it. It adds nothing to what we learn from Michael
Drosnin's book, but illustrates an important issue: just
because someone is good, it doesn't mean that they are
right.

That Mr Ramsbel is a good man is perfectly clear. It is
clear that he uses the Bible Code for the best possible
purposes – to draw people to the only One who can make
them perfectly happy. With Mr Ramsbel there is none of the
nonsense of alternative futures, nor does he have dates for
Armageddon!

He proves that a good man can make a good use of a bad
idea.

Anyone who has studied church history can compile a list of such errors.

Good men, bad ideas

We must not assume that good men are necessarily right. Nearly all the mistakes that can be made by good men have been. Mr Drosnin makes the sad mistake of trying to date his Armageddon, but John Wesley, the great gospel preacher, did the same!

John Wesley issued his *Notes on the New Testament* in 1754.[1] At the end of his comments on Revelation he summarises it all with dates. The date for 'the end' and the 'imprisonment of Satan' is 1836!

Another example is Clement, a leader in the early church mentioned in Philippians 4:3. He wrote a little booklet which, although never seen as Scripture, was favourite reading in the early church. Much of what he says is very helpful but, alas, he shows his belief in the ancient legend of the Phoenix, which was thought to return to life after death.[2]

In fact it seems that the mistakes of the very best men have done the worst damage. Rather than assess their views, Christians took them on faith. Their respect for the truly great stopped them testing the ideas against the Bible.

Not many great leaders have been able to resist the temptation of stating their opinions with great confidence. Anyone who has read John Calvin's commentaries on the Bible will admire his clarity and insight. He covered virtually the whole Bible, including all but one of the books of the New Testament. But perhaps his wisest act was *not* to write a commentary on Revelation!

---

[1] My copy published by the Wesleyan-Methodist Bookroom, no date (but old).

[2] 1 Clement 25.

John Wesley's is not the only old commentary on that difficult book which is embarrassing today. Perhaps they should have imitated Calvin, and kept to what they knew!

The thing is, we are all subject to mistakes. To be made good and holy is a great miracle, but it doesn't make our opinions infallible.

I believe that Christians should pay close attention to what their leaders say. But evangelicals have no infallible pope; we test what we are told by the infallible words of the Bible. This is harder work than simply being told what to believe, but it is vital. The Bible tells us: 'Test all things; hold fast what is good' (1 Thessalonians 5:21). 'Beloved, do not believe every spirit, but test the spirits, whether they are of God; because many false prophets have gone out into the world' (1 John 4:1).

The Bible Code comes to us with the weight of authorities: scientists, computer experts and computers. But we cannot set our common sense aside. Lists of powerful names are no substitute for real evidence and true logic. In fact, those who sense that their case is weak make most use of the authorities to make their case.

But we will not be steamrollered into believing the Bible Code. We have not forgotten our suspicions that there is a cover-up behind all this, but what is it? What don't they want us to see?

We unearth the real agenda in the next chapter.

5
The Heart of the Matter

So now we come to it: what is really going on? Is there a cover-up, and if so, of what? What does the system not want us to believe, and what is it using as a smokescreen?

To understand what is going on, we need to go back two or three centuries. Philosophers were once again trying to build a philosophy without God.

Why would anyone want to do that?

Applying for the vacant throne

From the very beginning, mankind wanted God's job. The original temptation was to 'be like God' (Genesis 3:5). Boiled down, this means selfishness, self-centredness and pride. We all need a focus, a principle, on which to live our lives. If God is that focus, then we are bound to obey him. That means living for *his* glory, not ours. It also means loving people we may not like.

But if there were no God, then I would have to find another focus. What better to serve as a focus than myself?

So behind 'I don't believe in God' lies 'I am my own god'. Of course one doesn't have to *say*, 'I am my own god.' It sounds so ridiculous to do so that it is better merely to say that one believes in nothing. All that matters is that I am living for me. Rather than love my neighbour, I find him useful. I may want his money or his wife, so I just help myself. Then again, I may want his respect and liking, so I am nice. I may even convince myself that I am an unselfish person.

The fact remains, though, that *I* am the centre of my life.

It isn't God's non-existence that mankind wants – it's his job.

This belief system is called humanism. It is sometimes regarded as a religion, which in many ways it is. But usually the true situation is covered over with a layer of words. The humanist is regarded as simply the ordinary person. He says he doesn't believe in God, or if he does, it is *his* idea of God – a 'god' of his own making. He says that he is 'objective' about the world religions, and thinks that everyone is entitled to their own opinion. In reality, he will not examine the proofs of Christianity. When he is shown remarkable confirmations of the truth of the Bible, his first reaction is to explain them away.

Why don't humanists simply admit what they believe? It is because the belief system is so ridiculous. It goes entirely against common sense. How can we be so important, like a god, when we have none of God's attributes? Mankind is so ungodlike! We do not choose to be born, nor can we prolong our lives at will, try as we may. We cannot control the chance events that affect us; we cannot know the future – as the Bible Code so graphically illustrates. We cannot even control our inner feelings, otherwise there would not be such a high incidence of depression and anxiety.

We cannot create anything as magnificent as ourselves. We are wonderfully made, but clearly we are not designed to be gods.

What is more, most people have an inner sense that there is a real God. This was the problem that the new humanistic philosophy had to face.

Kant's solution

There is no real answer to the problem, but an eighteenth-century philosopher found a convenient solution. He divided reality into two halves. One half was everything material, things you could measure and touch. In this realm, he said, we should use logic and scientific thought.

The other half was the 'spiritual' realm. Here we were not to use logical thought, but follow irrational impulses and intuitive hunches. Kant separated these two halves, and didn't allow them to spill over into one another.

His idea was so acceptable that most people still follow it, at least to some degree. It seems to solve the problem.

Mankind loves to be logical. Kant allowed that, but restricted it to the scientific realm. People were so good at it that it brought us into the amazing technological revolution of our day. Logic seemed to belong with things that could be measured; the supernatural was illogical, by definition.

So what about God? Here Kant's approach worked even better. Since God belonged, Kant said, to the 'spiritual' realm, it was no good being logical about him. People could ignore the proofs of God and the Bible, because proof didn't matter in this realm. Instead, they could have the most ridiculous beliefs, as long as these felt 'spiritual' and satisfied their instincts and intuitions.

This is why you get the two extremes today. There are some people who don't accept that anything exists unless they can test it in a laboratory. Since the all-powerful God could never be pinned down under a microscope, they feel justified in not believing in him. Logically, they shouldn't believe that they have love, or ambition, or indeed anything that makes them truly human! After all, what colour is love when you put it under a microscope? This is the extreme materialist. He is completely protected from knowing God, however much proof there might be.

The other extreme is the highly religious person, who uses no logic at all in his beliefs. He can believe anything, however ludicrous. For him it is enough that an idea occurs to him and feels right. If it is accompanied by a religious experience, it *must* be true. He is closed to any rational assessment of his beliefs, and easily prey to the devil's deceptions. This is the classic 'New-ager', but people of this sort can be found in churches too.

Most people are a combination of the two. When it comes to real life issues, they are rational and follow common sense; when it comes to science, they take great pains to follow each step with precise logic. But when the same people think about spiritual things, they adopt a completely different approach. They are intuitive, impulsive, illogical and mystical. They adopt a view of God that they cannot defend; they never expect to have to. All this, they think, is outside the realm of straight thinking.

It seemed that the problem was solved. Kant had found a way for man to ignore the proofs for the real God, and fill the gap with whatever religious view he chose. But of course there was one great difficulty: all this was entirely opposed to common sense. This is how the Bible begins: 'In the beginning God created the heavens and the earth' (Genesis 1:1). And this must be part of any understanding of God. By definition, he is the Creator and Controller of everything that is.

Common sense rebels at separating the Designer from his design and making them belong to two entirely different realms. How can I have nothing to do with what I have made? It is quite the reverse in real life. The things that people 'create' – such as songs and stories – reveal something of who these people are. In fact, that is why they 'create' – to express some deep part of themselves.

So Kant's artificially divided universe was always

threatening to collapse under the weight of its own irrationality.

Enter the Bible Code

Something had to be found which would satisfy common sense. And since nothing does, other than the truth, there had to be several 'solutions'. As each solution proves useless, something new takes its place, and so on.

One such solution is the 'science proves the supernatural' approach. There are many examples of this. In Victorian times it became fashionable to interact with evil spirits using 'scientific' methods. This was called 'psychic research'. People have always known that there are evil spirits, but of course they could not be allowed in Kant's 'scientific' realm. Now psychic research seemed to connect what had become separated.

But the connection was only superficial. People were not being rational about God and the Bible. They had merely applied scientific method to a tiny aspect of the supernatural.

This sort of thing cannot really satisfy, so each fashion dies out, to be replaced by something new. We have already mentioned Erich Von Daniken, whose *Chariots of the Gods?* made a powerful impression a few years ago.[1] In it he 'proved' that some of the supernatural events of the past really happened. Ezekiel's vision *was* reality, but it had nothing to do with God. It was really alien spacemen. Von Daniken's 'proofs' have long since been discredited, but the book satisfied an inner need. It seemed to bring the logical world of science into the world of spiritual things.

The Bible Code is just more of the same. It seems to deal in scientific things – it is all computers and the sayings of

---

[1] Bantam Books, 1971.

scientists – but what it deals with belongs to Kant's 'spiritual' realm: predictions, the end of the world, the Bible.

No wonder the Bible Code is so popular! It is the latest temporary healing of the rift between Kant's two realms. It will all be forgotten in a few years, as all the others have been, but meanwhile the reader thrills as the Bible and complex mathematical calculations jostle together on the same page. We hear about Armageddon and miraculous predictions, and then we are with expert code-breakers and impressive statistics.

The Bible Code is part of an enormous cover-up. It is an inoculation to keep us from wondering why we can't apply logic to 'spiritual' matters.

But suppose we refuse to be misled? What would happen if we ignored the system and followed common sense?

The key to life

G. K. Chesterton remarked that life is a funny old thing, and the key to it will be a funny shape too. But don't be put off, said Chesterton. Use the key that fits, however strange it may seem to you.

The most amazing event in history is the resurrection of Jesus Christ. That it really happened is a matter of faith, but also of logic. Let us start with the logic.

How do we know that something has happened? Circumstantial evidence helps, but the main thing is the witnesses. This is what you need in witnesses:

● That they are in a position really to *know* the truth of what they say.
● That they have no reason to lie about it.
● That they are numerous enough to remove all doubt.

These are common-sense requirements. Suppose someone has been arrested for burgling a house. The witnesses must have been close enough to see him. It helps if they already know him – after all, it is easy to mistake a total stranger. They must have no reason to lie, so if they are known to hate him, their testimony loses some of its force. Again, if there is just one witness, it is not ideal. You don't need hundreds of witnesses – three or four good ones will do. And finally, something should be missing from the house.

These requirements are remarkably fulfilled in the witnesses to Christ's resurrection. The witnesses knew Jesus very well – they had spent three years in intimate fellowship with him. They spent a month with him after he rose from the dead: '...to whom He also presented Himself alive after His suffering by many infallible proofs, being seen by them during forty days' (Acts 1:3). It is quite impossible that they could have been mistaken. They knew he had died; they knew he was buried. They saw him regularly and intimately after his resurrection. They witnessed his resurrection body which was able to walk through walls, and yet could also eat and be touched. They could see that he had not merely been resuscitated. They could see that it was really him.

'Ah, yes,' says someone, 'but how do we know that they weren't lying?'

They had absolutely no reason to lie about it. Why do people give a false testimony? Sometimes the motive is money, sometimes fear of violence, sometimes malice. Now just look at these witnesses! They made no money from their testimony – in fact they lost all they had. Their property was forfeit, their freedom taken away. They were insulted, abused and tortured. They had to trust God for the essentials of physical life. And all because of their testimony! You couldn't get rich out of Christianity in those days.

And far from saving them from violence, their testimony brought violence upon them. Some gave their lives rather than say that their testimony was untrue. Although people will sometimes die for a mistaken belief, these men died for their testimony to Christ's resurrection concerning which they could not have been mistaken.

What is more, these men believed that 'all liars shall have their part in the lake which burns with fire and brimstone, which is the second death' (Revelation 21:8). They had no reason to lie at all. To do so, they believed, would mark them as hell-bound.

Nor are we talking about just one or two witnesses. There were eleven intimate witnesses, plus many others: 'He was seen by over five hundred brethren at once, of whom the greater part remain to the present' (1 Corinthians 15:6). We have the testimony in the four gospels, and throughout the New Testament.

Finally, there was the tomb with the missing body. No one could produce it – not the Romans, nor the Jews, nor the disciples.

The apostles couldn't be mistaken; they couldn't be lying. Unless someone is already prejudiced, he is bound to accept that no historical event will have better witnesses than these. It is only logical to accept that Jesus really did rise from the dead, as the New Testament describes.

Where does that lead us?

Jesus and the Bible

The same witnesses who confirm Jesus' resurrection also record his deeds and teaching. We can be as sure about these as we should be about the resurrection. After three years of ministry, Jesus was executed as a criminal. But he claimed to be the Son of God, ie God the Son, come to earth as a human. His resurrection substantiated his claim.

After all, only the direct power of God could lie behind the resurrection. So since God raised Jesus, it follows that what he did and taught is right.

In particular Jesus absolutely affirmed the Old Testament (Matthew 5:17–19), and miraculously equipped his apostles to write the New Testament (John 16:12–14). The whole Bible, therefore, has his divine authorisation. So there is no logic in believing in Jesus on the one hand but not the Bible on the other.

Jesus' resurrection is a unique event. No resuscitation or miraculous healing compares to it, because his resurrection body is unlike anything ever known. No clearer proof could be had that his teaching is true. After all, the resurrection is the ultimate divine affirmation. How could it happen to someone who misled people about God?

The point I am making is this: once you have absorbed the evidence for the resurrection, you are bound by common sense to accept the Bible. You can't, for instance, say that Jesus was merely a good man. Had that been all he was, he would have been a deceiver, since he claimed that 'all authority in heaven and on earth' was given to him (Matthew 28:18).

It may sound acceptably 'spiritual' to speak of Jesus as a mere human, a teacher, a spiritual leader. But it is quite contrary to common sense. If someone has a grossly exaggerated view of who they are, how can they be 'spiritual'? If someone (wrongly) thinks they are God, what is the point of listening to *anything* they have to say? It does no good to evade this by saying that such high claims were wrongly attributed to him, because we have already established that the witnesses are irreproachable.

In spite of this, it is all too common in academic circles for theologians to find fault with the Bible. Even more amazingly, they regard Bible-believers as 'fundamentalists' – people who lack rationality and intellectual consistency.

For such, the very idea that the Bible is God's book is unacceptable.

Surely true rationality and spirituality combine in the person who realises that Jesus Christ is life's only sure guide.

Coming into the light

The person who wants to know the logic in Christian belief should make an honest study of the evidence for Jesus' resurrection. If the resurrection really happened, then one must believe in Jesus, or abandon common sense for ever.

There is no equivalent miracle in other belief systems. Humanism has absolutely no rational basis at all. Muhammad and Joseph Smith (the founders of Islam and the Mormons respectively) were given their vital revelations by angels, and there is no evidence either that this really happened or, if it did, that the angels were good angels. The details of Buddha's life are in some doubt, and in any case, he lacks any divine accreditation. Jesus Christ is utterly unique.

There are those who have come to faith in Jesus through examining the evidence for the resurrection. One such person was Frank Morison, a high court judge, who set out to disprove Christianity by discrediting the resurrection. He ended up disproving *himself*. He tells the full story in *Who Moved the Stone?*.[1]

But this is rare. Most people avoid looking at disagreeable facts. If they are told them, they don't give them a fair hearing, but are out to dismiss them by any means available. The reason for this is that Kant was entirely wrong. There are not two distinct realms of logic

---

[1]Published by Faber and Faber, 1967. Currently published by OM Publishing.

and spirituality. There are just people. Their spiritual state (their standing with God) and their rational processes are intimately connected. Although people talk about being objective and unbiased, this may just be self-delusion.

> And this is the condemnation, that the light has come into the world, and men loved darkness rather than light, because their deeds were evil. For everyone practicing evil hates the light and does not come to the light, lest his deeds should be exposed. But he who does the truth comes to the light, that his deeds may be clearly seen, that they have been done in God (John 3:19–21).

If people are determined not to 'come to the light', no amount of logic will force them. Christians are advised not to rely on the power of logic in their efforts to help those around them. It is one thing to win an argument, but quite another to see someone's mind changed. The chains of sin are very strong. I have often seen people silenced by the force of logic while remaining unchanged. More often they are just cross at having lost a contest. The thought of approaching the all-powerful God never, it seems, occurs to them.

It is just as wrong, however, to rely on non-rational inducements. I have seen people deeply impressed with powerful spiritual experiences or miracles, and still not come to a true faith in Christ.

The fact is, it is God who draws people to himself: 'No one can come to Me,' said Jesus, 'unless the Father who sent Me draws him' (John 6:44). God uses his people. As we see in the Acts of the Apostles, praying is a great part of that, and so is a clear logical statement of God's message.

A true change of mind and heart is a miraculous event. What is needed 'is the exceeding greatness of His power toward us who believe, according to the working of His mighty power which He worked in Christ when He raised

Him from the dead and seated Him at His right hand in the
heavenly places' (Ephesians 1:19–20). Nothing less than
resurrection power can change us.

The cover-up

This brings the main question before us: Who is covering up
what and why? The answer is that the system is covering
up the truth about God and man. The motive is that they
don't want to know it themselves, and they certainly don't
want the masses to know it either. They would rather sit on
God's 'vacant' throne, and live their lives as if they were
under no higher authority. They don't want any God to
prohibit their freedom to sin. They don't want the people
they control to come to God either. This would bring
another, and higher, authority into play, and their own
control would be lessened. They would have to justify
themselves to others. They realise that this is very hard,
impossible really, when people are learning God's ways.

How do they do it? Their main weapon is never to
mention the relevant data. 'Religious' issues are covered in
schools and through the media, but never properly. The
evidence for the resurrection is never exhibited.
'Christianity' is covered by information on religious
buildings and other secondary issues. Any disagreements
within the churches are publicised, particularly any
immorality among the ministers.

And lest the people begin to crave true spirituality, they
are fed an endless diet of irrationalities – New Age
revelations and superstitions. For the more 'scientifically'
minded, there is the Bible Code and similar wonders.

In the midst of all this, nobody is supposed to guess that
the most stupendous data is suppressed.

This explains why *The Bible Code* discounts the Bible
from time to time. It would be more logical, from the

standpoint of the Bible Code, if the Bible were read with interest and respect. After all, as we saw in Chapter 2, it would make better sense for the same Bible to be valuable as both code *and* book.

We saw in the last chapter that Yacov Ramsbel supports both Bible *and* Bible Code. Why didn't the system promote a book by someone like him? Why do we find the bestseller comes from Mr Drosnin, a man with no interest in the Bible?

The reason is now clear. We are being fed the Bible Code to take our minds off the Bible. So far as the system is concerned, that is the purpose of it all.

Undeceptions

To some of us it seems strange that Jesus Christ should be the key to life. As Chesterton would say, it is a strangely shaped key! But in Christ everything makes sense. Rational common sense and spiritual faith come together in him.

We go to the Bible because the best witnesses you could have show us that it represents the truth. We see that the fact of the resurrection undergirds all its statements. Our minds cleared of the popular prejudice, we delve into this remarkable book. We find an amazing depth and an unassuming simplicity.

As C. H. Spurgeon said, it is like a river in which an elephant can swim, and yet a lamb can paddle. The simplest person can read the Bible and learn, and the greatest brains find the depths utterly unfathomable. The Bible is a miracle beyond the wildest fantasies of the Bible Code!

But alongside this intellectual satisfaction there is a spiritual witness. Just as the truest logic is found in the Bible, so are the most genuine spiritual experiences. The experiences of those who read the Bible in faith are indescribable. No wonder they love to read it every day or several times a day.

The witness of the Spirit of God is like an old-fashioned seal. In times past, a man would put hot wax on a document and then press his ring into it. His coat-of-arms, which was on the ring, was then clearly seen on the wax. This was his seal. The image of the coat-of-arms would not be perfectly reproduced in the wax, but it would be there, and it would be clearer to see than if one just looked at his ring.

When believers experience the Spirit of God, they are not given revelations of God beyond the Bible. They feel what they read. Their feelings are not as accurate as the infallible Bible, but they make the words of the Bible powerfully alive and applicable. Simple expressions like 'your sins are forgiven' are felt with enormous force. They feel that they *know* that this is God's book. The logic and the spiritual experience form a beautiful whole.

Where does all this lead us? If we work logically from this point, we shall be in for a few shocks. The church has not escaped the influence of the system. We *all* need to think about the issues raised by the Bible Code.

Having arrived at the heart of the matter, and laid a rational/spiritual foundation, it is time to start building and see where we shall arrive.

This is the task of the chapters that follow.

6
Secret Revelations

In the realm of sensational books the notion of 'secret revelations' is very powerful. To those who like such things, it seems all too likely that there should be a secret, hidden in obscurity, that explains everything.

It is sufficiently clear that most people do not have the secret of life. So they imagine that this vital secret must be hidden in some obscure place, where most people cannot find it.

The 'secret revelation' books find the ancient knowledge in some hidden tomb, or in the mathematical arrangement of a pyramid. The new revelation is thus a blend of ancient and modern: 'It was always there, but we needed modern technology to find it.' The Bible Code fits the familiar pattern.

Very often it is the less technological cultures that supply the missing key. It is the American Indians with their ancient and simple lifestyle, or perhaps the Druids of pre-Christian England. These peoples are little known to most of us, and it is easier to believe that they have the key which we lack.

The question is, why did the key disappear? Why was it hidden in a tomb and forgotten by the rest of the world if it really *was* the key? If the Druids had it, why did they fade away? Shouldn't everyone have seen their contentment and begged them for enlightenment?

Some laugh at the whole business. 'There is no key!' they say. 'Just get on with real life.' But a deeply felt optimism stops us from doing that. There must be an answer.

After all, we live in a world of marvels. Science continually brings astonishing things to light. And we sense that mankind is a mighty miracle – even if things aren't going very well for us. There just *has* to be a solution!

Living in the midst of all these miracles, can it be that we are meant to be so isolated, aimless, depressed, suicidal, selfish, dishonest, frustrated and fed up? Even if you are not any of these, you know plenty of people who are.

The Bible Code, of course, touches this deep sense within us. But we have seen that it is part of a cover-up to take our minds off the real thing.

The Bible itself is the hidden revelation.

Hidden and public

The Bible fits perfectly with what we are looking for. It *is* a hidden revelation in that most people have no idea what is in it. On the other hand, it has never been forgotten, discarded or hidden in a cave. It is right there, in the centre of life, completely visible and yet ignored.

The Bible was written over a period of 1,500 years, by public figures. Some, like Moses, David, Solomon and Daniel, were leaders in their nations. Others, like Jeremiah, James and Peter, were 'nobodies'. But these nobodies were well known – sufficiently prominent to be persecuted by the mob.

As it was being written, the Bible became public property. Its books were copied and made available to anyone who wanted them. They were never part of any secret tradition like some of the 'secret revelations' discovered today. What motive is there to keep the key to life a secret? It must mean that the key may collapse under scrutiny, or perhaps that the enlightened are too selfish to enlighten others!

The public nature of the Bible is a great advantage. Many of its writers are known from secular history, and there is no possibility that the things they relate are imaginary.

Many authors contributed to the Bible. No human edited or co-ordinated their contributions, so the amazing harmony of the Bible defies any explanation other than the obvious – that God brought it into being. Once the Old Testament was complete, it was translated into Greek, and thus made available to the Mediterranean world. The New Testament likewise was soon spread through the world in a variety of translations.

But despite it being open and public, the Bible is a secret book in our culture today.

Covers and contents

We see Bibles pretty often. They are used in law courts, but not opened. You see them in bookshops, sometimes in 'christening editions'. These are small and prettily bound copies of the Bible: too small to read conveniently, but nice to hold. The Bible sometimes crops up in general knowledge, and can be heard (mis)quoted in movies. Such references usually display how little people know of it. The cover of the Bible is familiar; the contents are not.

Of course, the Bible is prominent in the church. Some churches have huge editions of the Bible at the front. Others are specifically 'Bible-based' and operate in a 'biblical' manner. The fact that this is mentioned implies that other churches appear not to be so biblical.

My question at this point, however, is whether the Bible is well known even in 'biblical' churches. Do Bible-based Christians really know what the Bible contains? My suspicion is that all too often they do not. The cover, yes; certain parts of it, maybe; all of it, apparently not.

What has all this to do with the Bible Code? My point is that the Bible Code is part of a cover-up. If you don't know the Bible particularly well, then it seems that the cover-up is working.

'But I *could* read the Bible, if I set myself to it,' someone says. 'No one is stopping me; I just haven't been getting round to it.'

Of course no one is being physically stopped. That isn't how a cover-up works. The disinclination to study the Bible among those who know that it is God's book is one of the great mysteries of our day. The covers are on public display; the contents are a secret. Let us see what this means in practice.

I am referring to those of us who know that the Bible is from God. We know that God has revealed himself in the Bible; his character and nature are there, his style and how he does things. Even on the human scale creators express something of themselves in their creation. With God it is more emphatically so. He didn't bring this universe into existence in order to abandon it in darkness. His motives are loving and kind, however firm he is with rebels and insurrectionists.

Why not reveal himself within our minds? Would this not have been easier than arranging for the Bible to be written, preserved, translated and distributed? Easier it would have been, but not so effective. God permits the devil to tempt people within their minds. This is necessary so that lovers of God choose him over all other pleasures and good things. But it means that the mind is a battlefield. Whatever intimations of truth are there, they are all too easily muddled with deceptions. But God didn't want to make a dubious revelation of himself. The truth had to be revealed in an unmistakable fashion so that the most confused could hear his voice.

The Bible is the perfect answer.

The message

What is in the Bible? There are two essential revelations: what God is like, and what we are like. Both revelations are indispensable. If I don't know the nature of the true God, then how will I avoid the fakes? 'False christs and false prophets will rise,' Jesus warned, 'and show great signs and wonders to deceive, if possible, even the elect' (Matthew 24:24).

The issue is not the mere name: my 'Christ' may not be the true Christ. If I seek a Christ who is different in nature from the biblical Jesus Christ, then I am sure to be deceived. If I do not know how God reveals himself throughout the Bible, I am at terrible risk.

There are so many mistakes that can be made about God! No simple formula can correct our natural bent to make our own image of God. God tells us all we need to know in the Bible.

It is crucial likewise that I know who *I* am. Again, the name is not the vital thing. It is no good if I approach God, and the 'me' who does so isn't real. If I imagine myself to be good enough for God, then I don't know myself. A disastrous element of unreality has been introduced. To know myself I need to get past the all-pervading human practice of self-deception: 'The heart is deceitful above all things, and desperately wicked; who can know it? I, the LORD, search the heart, I test the mind' (Jeremiah 17:9–10). As the Bible-reader grows in the knowledge of God, he learns more about himself. The good news of God's grace easily outweighs the bad news of mankind's true state.

Promises and commands

The Bible, we know, contains God's amazing promises. These promises cover everything good – physical, social and spiritual. We know that Christians live by faith in these promises, so obviously we need to know what these promises are.

'Need to know' makes it sound like a dull duty. Surely it is anything but that! How many of us would like to browse our favourite catalogue, knowing that everything in there was ours for the asking? If mere material things arouse such desire within us, surely divine things are much more desirable!

The Bible is no mere catalogue, of course. That is far too impersonal an image. God is intimately involved with us. He doesn't give us something we think we need if it isn't the best thing for us. 'We know that all things work together for good to those who love God, to those who are the called according to His purpose' (Romans 8:28).

When God makes a promise to us in the Bible, it is not automatic. We are told to ask for what he promises. Many examples of this asking come in the Bible. The point is, we need to *know* what is promised, trust the promise, and make our request specifically. These are things that are impossible if we don't know the Bible. How many promises are unfulfilled in our lives simply because we didn't know they were there?

The Bible also contains God's rule of life. These are the commands of the Bible, and what a great gift they are too. All too often we have taken the wrong road, made the wrong choices and suffered the consequences. It wasn't that we were out to do the wrong thing – we just needed guidance. The perfect map of life is in the Bible.

Some people seem to think that God's pattern for life is too simple. 'You just have to love,' they say, 'and that's it.' But is love so simple? If you love someone, you want to make them happy. But how can I make someone happy if I don't know what they want? I may buy them a CD, but choose one they don't like. I may try to help them, but it's in an area where they like to do things on their own.

In short, love is just the beginning. 'If you love Me,' said Jesus, 'keep My commandments' (John 14:15). Love is the motivation; the commandments are the expression.

But how can I love Jesus if I don't try to learn what pleases him? Knowing the whole Bible is vital.

The smokescreen

It isn't as if it is particularly difficult to get to know the Bible. Anyone familiar with the history of the church knows that it used to be better known. The Authorised Version of the Bible was so familiar that it changed the English language. It wasn't just the stories of the Bible that people knew. Most people find the prophets harder to understand, but these were known too. The familiar expression 'holier than thou', for instance, is from the prophet Isaiah (65:5, AV).

Do we know the prophets? What is the message of Zephaniah? What had Micah to say? How about the books of Moses (Genesis to Deuteronomy)? Do we know how God set up his Old Testament nation? Do we read Job or Ecclesiastes? This is not an attempt to make the Christian feel guilty. Let's forget all that for the moment. There is a mystery here, and we are right in the centre of it. The clues are all within our minds; we are the victims of the cover-up. Rather than feel guilty, we should feel cheated. We have been duped. The question is: Are we going to do something about it?

I remember, as a child, being fooled over and over again by the same card trick. I felt that if I could watch it one more time, surely I would spot how it was done! In the end I had to beg for the truth! When I realised how simple it was, I felt rather foolish. How had I failed to spot that? There is something far more serious than card tricks here.

The most important issues are at stake. Our very souls are being sabotaged. Why should we let the system do it any longer?

God has gone to amazing lengths to make his words available to us in the Bible. Are we going to let the system snatch them away? The first thing is to understand how it is done. Now is the time to apply the things we have been looking at so far.

In Chapter 5 we saw how Kant separated reality into two artificial halves. This was part of the cover-up. How does it apply to our reading of the Bible? There are two answers to this, depending on whether we are on the 'scientific' side or the 'spiritual'.

Rational irrationality

We have already mentioned that Kant's 'scientific' realm led to sceptics within the church. These are called 'liberals' since they have 'liberated' themselves from following God in order to devise a way of their own. For liberals, it is unthinkable that the miraculous events in the Bible actually took place. Not that they put it that way. They simply state the 'real' explanation of a miracle, and trust in the power of Kant's scientific realm to convince their hearers.

When I studied for my first theology degree, I was deeply impressed by the power these men had to make me ashamed of the miracles in the Bible. Then one kindly professor spilled the beans. 'Why,' he asked, 'do you think modern scholars discount the miracles of the Bible?' We were speechless – it had never occurred to us to ask the question. 'It is because,' he said in his precise manner, 'miracles are *assumed* to be impossible.'

I remember heaving a great sigh of relief. It was a moment of enlightenment. The great weight of scholarly authority had been pressing so hard upon me, and now it dissipated like the morning mist. It wasn't their knowledge or expertise, merely their prejudices and unbelief, that made them oppose the Bible. That professor belonged to their number, but I shall always be grateful to him for being so honest about it.

Another professor was not so candid. To downgrade the Bible, liberals often teach that the books of Moses were forged more than a thousand years after his time. But in my studies I came across the fact that the Samaritans had the same books of Moses as the Jews. Samaritans and Jews had been at odds for several centuries before the time liberals say the books were written. How could they share the same sacred books?

I was reluctant to accept the biblical view of things as I was still prejudiced in favour of liberalism. But when I asked my Hebrew professor, I was astonished at his answer. There were no reasons given, no rational arguments advanced. All he said was: 'That's fundamentalism, Philip!' He just about cured me of liberalism with a couple of words!

The liberal bias lurks in the minds of many Christians. As they read the Bible, they feel that it would be too naive and unsophisticated simply to believe. Instead of thinking about the risen Christ, they are continually obstructed by liberalism. Easily answered doubts prey upon them, and they lose the intimacy of God in the Bible. All too often their ministers increase their distress by teaching them the liberalism with which they themselves have been indoctrinated. Or sometimes, these Christians feel too guilty to mention their doubts, afraid that they will be dubbed heretics. Clearly there will be little joy in Bible reading until they understand the basis for the Bible's authority. That's the place to clear the smokescreen. Such people need to ask themselves why Christians have always believed the Bible to be God's book. They need to go back to Christ and his witness to Scripture. This is a matter of rational research, and also for prayer. Overcoming deception is not as easy as it sounds. It is the work of the Holy Spirit to establish the truth in our hearts. Never underestimate the work of the Holy Spirit.

I knew a minister who had been thoroughly indoctrinated in liberalism. He found himself in a prayer meeting where he suddenly became aware of God's power and the presence of the Holy Spirit. He told me later that *all* the liberalism left him in a moment. He became a clear preacher of God's truth. His indoctrination had taken several years yet he was undeceived in moments. Never underestimate the power of God. Never try to get along without it.

Once it is fixed in our minds that the Bible is God's book, we shall have a strong incentive to read it thoroughly. This is true rationality: once we know that God speaks to us in the Bible we gladly listen. The only reason not to read it is that we don't want to hear what he has to say.

Unspiritual spirituality

The other side of Kant's division works just as well, perhaps even better. In this realm the Christian feels that rationality plays little part in spiritual things. If God were to speak to mankind, he feels, it must be through intuitive means – direct voices, dreams, visions. He thinks that the mystic, rather than the Bible student, has the key to the revelation of God. Such a person will not discount the Bible like the liberal does. He agrees that it is God's book, but he thinks that there is a more direct way to hear God's voice. Bible study involves mental concentration; surely it is more spiritual to empty one's mind and hear God directly!

If such a person reads the Bible, he will do it in a mystical fashion. That is, he will not really think about what he has read. He will not compare it with other parts of the Bible, or analyse the actual words. He just reads, and hopes that a mystical experience will come. He doesn't read to learn, but to receive a spiritual experience. The parts of the Bible that don't yield such experiences are simply left unread. The other parts are read and re-read.

Perhaps the words of the Bible spark off an inner picture; if so, this becomes the 'personal revelation' that the person has received. The Bible has played a quite secondary role in it all. For instance, they read: 'Deliver yourself like a gazelle from the hand of the hunter, and like a bird from the hand of the fowler' (Proverbs 6:5). Perhaps the person is having difficulties with a Mr Fowler. They then interpret the passage accordingly. They feel that God has told them to get away from the influence of Mr Fowler. Clearly this is not the intended meaning of the text. Understood rationally, it warns us of those who act like 'fowlers', bird-catchers. It may be that Mr Fowler is one such, but then again, maybe not.

Obviously if we approach the Bible like that, we can get it to say anything we wish. People break their marriages, and disobey other clear commands of God, on this sort of pretext. 'God spoke to me,' they say, and then produce this sort of misread text. Has a *Mrs* Fowler ever abused this text to justify breaking her marriage, I wonder?

The point is, this is not a *rational* way to read the Bible. But the people who do it are prejudiced against rationality in spiritual things.

More often the cover-up works in this way. Christians are encouraged to believe that the most direct way to hear God is through a spiritual experience, apart from the Bible. What they really want is just such an experience. Reading the Bible seems a distant second best, so they don't do it with great expectations, nor very often.

Those who want spiritual experiences are reasonably

sure to get them, one way or another. 'Satan himself transforms himself into an angel of light' for just this purpose (2 Corinthians 11:14). Since they lack an all-round knowledge of the Bible, they have no defence against deception. When the call comes to 'not believe every spirit, but test the spirits, whether they are of God; because many false prophets have gone out into the world' (1 John 4:1) such people are helpless, but they don't know it. They search their memories for something in the Bible which would help, but the Bible isn't in their memories – only their favourite parts of it are.

For such people spiritual experiences become like a drug. The more they have, the more they need. They don't realise that it isn't spiritual experiences that they require: it's *genuine* spiritual experiences.

The answer to such a condition is to re-examine how God speaks to mankind. We need to remember that the Scriptures are God's infallible communication, *and nothing else is*! Our experiences need to be tested in a thorough and responsible manner. A spiritual experience may require hours of study if it is to be tested properly.

Once someone begins to do this, he realises that he has not sufficiently tested such things before. He needs to see what God says about deception in the Bible. He needs to remember that 'Jesus answered and said to them: "Take heed that no one deceives you. For many will come in My name, saying, 'I am the Christ,' and will deceive many"' (Matthew 24:4–5). Just because an inner voice identifies itself with Christ, it does not mean it really is, however powerful the spiritual experience that accompanies it.

When we see these things, Bible reading will become a matter of urgency, and then of joy. 'My sheep hear My voice, and I know them, and they follow Me' (John 10:27). Once we recognise Jesus' voice in the Bible, it is a great joy to listen and follow.

Once bitten, twice shy

If you see yourself to any degree in either of these characters, rejoice! You will have found Bible study difficult, but now you know why. You have been tricked and robbed. But if you've seen through it, you won't be had again.

Now is the time to put something solid in place. Indeed, we are overdue for changes within the churches. All such changes begin with the individual, and that means you and me.

If the Bible Code has made us rethink our view of the Bible, then it has done some good. Let us start doing something about it!

We go on now to see how we can experience the ultimate secret revelation: meeting God in his book.

7
Decoding the Bible

So far, we have examined the Bible Code and found that it is based on a number of contradictions. We have seen that the 'Bible' it uses is mutilated – only an unpronounceable and meaningless series of consonants remains.

We have asked ourselves why the Bible Code, and similar 'discoveries', were launched into bestselling sensations. And we found the reason: the system is strongly discouraging us from looking seriously at the Bible.

We have faced the mystery of why many 'Bible-believing' Christians know the Bible so comparatively little, and seen an answer in the power of the system to infiltrate even the church.

If we stopped here, however, it would all be for nothing. What would we have? Just a few interesting points to make whenever the Bible Code is being discussed. We would be as much manipulated by the system as we presently are.

Something has to change.

Our only protection

What is this system? The Bible word for it is 'the world'. 'The wisdom of this world is foolishness with God' (1 Corinthians 3:19). For all its pretensions, God sees it as mere 'foolishness'.

How can we be rid of this foolishness? This is easier said than done because the system is all-pervasive, and we cannot simply opt out of it. For one thing, it is so natural and ordinary to us. The world's way just seems like normality, the obvious view of things.

Something very powerful needs to happen if we are ever to be free of the system. This is what the Bible says:

> I beseech you therefore, brethren, by the mercies of God, that you present your bodies a living sacrifice, holy, acceptable to God, which is your reasonable service. And do not be conformed to this world, but be transformed by the renewing of your mind, that you may prove what is that good and acceptable and perfect will of God (Romans 12:1–2).

Here's the thing we are looking for: 'do not be conformed to this world'. The world cannot merely be removed – it must be replaced. It is impossible to have *nothing* in its place. Here we see the cure to the system's subtle manipulations: 'be transformed by the renewing of your mind'.

This transformation in our thinking comes from knowing the will of God. This in turn comes from knowing what the Bible says. This is a far bigger matter than most people realise.

For one thing, Kant's unnatural division of reality affects the very way people think about the Bible. It is thought that it deals with the 'religious' part of life – as if any part of life could be independent of the Creator! But, led by this misconception, people look in the Bible for guidance within narrow limits. When it comes to family life, business, entertainment, friendships, they don't think that God has much to tell them.

Nothing could be more wrong than this. Anyone, for instance, who looks at the book of Proverbs will find hardly anything about 'religious' matters at all. It is nearly all about 'secular' issues.

So we are looking for God's way in every area of life. But there is more to it than that. We need to read the Bible in a submissive frame of mind, as living sacrifices.

The first step in approaching the Bible

The fact is, we can't understand what is in the Bible without God's help. Not because it is too complex, but because we have an inner disposition to be our own gods. Humility, rather than intellectual brilliance, is what is needed.

This is one of the amazing things about the Bible. It isn't hard for the simple believer to read it and learn God's secrets, while the very same passages are read by the genius who, if he is humble, realises that endless depths lay unplumbed before him.

But the most learned theologian, if he lacks humble faith, understands nothing at all. Why is this? The Bible is not like any other book. It is God speaking to us. God is so dazzlingly great that arrogance on our part is sheer madness. But it is also a barrier between us and God. 'The humble He teaches His way' (Psalm 25:9), and he has designed the Bible accordingly.

What about the arrogant? 'Though the LORD is on high, yet He regards the lowly; but the proud He knows from afar' (Psalm 138:6).

We see the same thing in the men God used in writing the Bible. There were intellectual geniuses, such as Solomon and Paul, but many of the others were simple people, with little education. The apostles were mostly of this sort – fishermen and the like. David was a shepherd, and so was Amos.

The Bible is a miraculous book! How could a group of

such disparate people, writing over a period of about 1,500 years, produce such a unified book? The message and themes of the Bible all fit together amid its marvellous diversity.

Think how the Bible has become 'my favourite book' for people over countless centuries, and within every culture. It is not foreign to the Chinese – they long for it so much that fearless Bible smugglers bring them copies. The Bible can be found in Hindu, Buddhist and Muslim countries where, amid persecution, people find the true God through it.

So there is nothing peculiarly Western about the Bible. It is 'my book' only if I read it in true faith and humility.

What shall we find when we open this unique book? We find words, and each word – each letter – is absolutely vital.

Every jot and tittle

'For assuredly, I say to you,' said Jesus, with great emphasis, 'till heaven and earth pass away, one jot or one tittle will by no means pass from the law till all is fulfilled' (Matthew 5:18). The jot and tittle were the tiniest pen-strokes in the Hebrew Old Testament.

Every tiny bit matters.

We have seen how the Bible Code tries to remove the vowels and punctuation from the Bible. This is what the system is trying to do. If we must read the Bible, they want us to follow the general gist rather than look closely at every detail.

Some modern translations of the Bible give only the general idea of the Bible, as the translators see it. This is why I use the New King James Version; it makes a responsible attempt to translate the actual words of the Bible.

The same is sometimes true in modern-day sermons and Christian teaching. The Bible is referred to in a general way. But if the Bible is what Jesus says it is, surely we need to base our beliefs on it in a thorough and careful manner. Of course, there are times when we read the Bible in large sections, to get the gist, the overall theme. This way we get the context and flow of it. But we always come back to examine the very words. 'Man shall not live by bread alone, but by every word that proceeds from the mouth of God' (Matthew 4:4). If you want to submit to God, see how he plans to take care of you, it is through 'every word' of the Bible, not merely its general gist.

With that in mind, we begin to read – or do we? This is not something that happens automatically. We need to make sure that we really read the Bible, rather than merely talk about reading it. The words won't help us unless we read them, and they enter our minds.

We need to make time to *study* the Bible. Remember that this is the only infallible source of God's words. Fellow Christians have much to teach us, but everyone makes mistakes, so we can't afford to put our trust in anyone, least of all ourselves.

Are you downgrading sermons, someone asks? Certainly not. If they are biblical, then they add to our Bible reading life. It comes down to this: if you want to hear God, he will speak to you through his book.

How to understand the Bible

Words won't help us if we don't understand them. The Bible is not a magic formula, where the mere repetition of the words is like a spell. Jesus said that his words did no good where they weren't understood: 'When anyone hears the word of the kingdom, and does not understand it, then the wicked one comes and snatches away what was sown in his heart. This is he who received seed by the wayside' (Matthew 13:19).

But how can we understand it? If we are really

determined to obey God, that is the first step: 'If anyone
wills to do His will, he shall know concerning the doctrine,
whether it is from God or whether I speak on My own
authority' (John 7:17). Very often people have difficulty
understanding the Bible because they don't want to hear
certain things. They don't want to know that they have to
admit they are wrong and change. They prefer to think that
they are unable to understand the Bible – even to blame the
Bible for being obscure – rather than submit to the true and
living God.

So search your heart. Are you prepared to do whatever
God tells you in the Bible? Have you put the key to every
room in your life into his hands? May he change whatever
he wishes? If so, then you are reading the Bible with the
right attitude.

But even then there are plenty of difficulties! How can I
understand what I read? There are several answers to give:

1. God doesn't tell us everything at once

The Bible is God's *living* words. He is personally in charge
as we read it prayerfully. This is no static situation; God has
a plan for each of his children. Obviously he will not teach
us everything at once.

We can understand the Bible without understanding
everything in it. What is important is to grasp what we need
to know now. Very often there will be a sense that we
need to grasp something specific. One particular mystery
will present itself, and we feel that we need to pursue it
until we crack the puzzle.

With this in mind, we look at how God helps us to
understand his book.

2. The answer lies in the whole Bible

In normal life, we understand a person on their own terms.
It is unreasonable to take people's words in ways they don't

intend. The fact, therefore, that someone speaks English doesn't mean they use the words exactly as you do.

There is an American car sticker that I sometimes see in England. It says: 'Honk if you know Jesus.' In America, 'honk' means 'blow your car horn' but, alas, this is not necessarily the case in some parts of England. In the northern counties, 'honk' is associated with nauseous and queasy spasms. This makes the car sticker rather inappropriate in the north.

The point is that we need to understand words in the sense that they are meant.

It is the same with God. He defines his terms in the Bible – the whole Bible. This is absolutely essential. If God's words are interpreted in pagan terms, you get pagan meanings. An example might clarify things.

'The anointing which you have received from Him abides in you, and you do not need that anyone teach you; but as the same anointing teaches you concerning all things, and is true, and is not a lie, and just as it has taught you, you will abide in Him' (1 John 2:27). What does this mean? What does God mean by 'anointing'? In some church circles 'anointing' is jargon for 'a special experience of the Holy Spirit'. If we read the Bible in terms of modern-day slang, then the verse tells us that if we have an experience of the Spirit, we do not need to be taught. But this would contradict the rest of the Bible, and even this part, because it is a letter from the apostle John *teaching* his readers. If they don't need to be taught, why teach them?

The confusion occurs when we don't understand a Bible word in Bible terms. In the Bible, priests, lepers and some kings were anointed. Of these, it was the particular calling of the priest to teach (Malachi 2:7).

The meaning, then, is that the believer has a priestly calling similar to that of the Old Testament priest. How did the priest gain his knowledge of God's ways? It wasn't merely by an experience of the Holy Spirit, but also by means of study and discipline. The Christian is presumed, therefore, to learn in the same way.

I have chosen this example because the Bible verse is sometimes misunderstood and can be used to discourage Bible study.

Everything depends, then, on knowing how God uses a term in the whole Bible. The only way to do this is to study the whole Bible. Having the whole Bible on your computer is not the same thing! Being able to find verses on a computer is not the same as having a personal familiarity with the Bible. This familiarity gives us clues which we cannot get from our Bible computer program.

In my last year of theological college I studied the book of Revelation as a special project. But I didn't get anywhere. I realised that I could never understand the book without knowing the whole Bible to which it refers so often. So I determined to increase my poor knowledge of the Scriptures – and never stopped! Now if I am stuck over a verse, I know I need to see it in the light of the whole. I may need to follow words or phrases to other parts of the Bible, and *then* I will understand the initial verse.

3. God sends his Spirit

The work of the Holy Spirit is absolutely vital if we are to understand God. The Bible is no dead letter, but living words from a living God. The Holy Spirit is powerfully at work as we try to understand it.

Although there is a great deal of emphasis on the Spirit bringing experiences, this is not his primary role, according to the Bible. In fact, to see the Holy Spirit as a giver of irrational experiences fits better with Kant.

In the Bible the Holy Spirit is revealed as the source of the Christ-like life. Wherever he is he produces 'love, joy, peace, longsuffering, kindness, goodness, faithfulness, gentleness,

self-control' (Galatians 5:22–23). As well as that, he helps
our mental processes:

> The Spirit of the LORD shall rest upon Him,
> The Spirit of wisdom and understanding,
> The Spirit of counsel and might,
> The Spirit of knowledge and of the fear of the LORD.
> His delight is in the fear of the LORD,
> And He shall not judge by the sight of His eyes,
> Nor decide by the hearing of His ears.
>
> (Isaiah 11:2–3).

This passage refers primarily to Jesus Christ, and only to us
as in him. But the point is that the work of the Holy Spirit is
mostly on the understanding. Look at what he gives:

'wisdom and understanding'
'counsel'
'knowledge and the fear of the LORD'.

The result of the Spirit's work is that the man 'judges' with
greater-than-human wisdom.

It is this wisdom we need in order to understand what
God is saying. The wonderful news is that God gives us the
Holy Spirit freely: 'how much more will your heavenly
Father give the Holy Spirit to those who ask Him!' (Luke
11:13).

This is why God says that the humble understand the
Bible, while the arrogant, however intellectual, can't. Only
the humble will recognise their need; only the humble truly
yearn for help; only the humble live in the Holy Spirit.

4. God sends teachers

The Holy Spirit works powerfully through the teachers God
sends. If God didn't send teachers, then people would
inevitably put all the emphasis on what they feel within.

They would be left to themselves to judge what is and what isn't the guidance of the Holy Spirit within.

This would be highly dangerous. We, in our arrogance, assume that we are right. But God warns that there are deceptive spirits about, and that we can easily be deceived: 'Now the Spirit expressly says that in latter times some will depart from the faith, giving heed to deceiving spirits and doctrines of demons' (1 Timothy 4:1).

Of course, human teachers can deceive as well, but there is more opportunity to test the human we can see. For instance, Jesus warned of false prophets, and said that 'by their fruits you will know them' (Matthew 7:20). Although the whole truth may not be known until much later, there are often clues. There are famous teachers who have been caught out in immorality, or who are known to teach heresy in more private settings. It is possible to get this sort of information about people, but we can never get it about spirits.

To the teachers God says:

> Preach the word! Be ready in season and out of season. Convince, rebuke, exhort, with all longsuffering and teaching. For the time will come when they will not endure sound doctrine, but according to their own desires, because they have itching ears, they will heap up for themselves teachers; and they will turn their ears away from the truth, and be turned aside to fables (2 Timothy 4:2–4).

No serious student of the Bible will turn from 'sound doctrine'. He will long for true and faithful explanations of the Bible. He will want the Bible applied to actual life, even if it means painful 'rebukes'.

Thank God for the great teachers of the past! Though dead, they continue to speak through their books. If you have the great Bible teachers sitting on your bookshelf, you will never be without help.

A true minister of Jesus Christ doesn't say: 'Believe what I tell, because I tell you.' His authority comes from the Bible, so he demonstrates the truth of his words by appealing to Scripture. Once he has shown you where the verses are, you can judge for yourself whether or not he is right.

I advise people to read the Bible teachers of the past. Why? Because the Bible was better known then, on every level. The really great figures are all in the past, although we pray that all this will one day change. Of course life has altered a great deal over the years, and a magnificent teacher like C. H. Spurgeon (nineteenth century) did not have television, computers and modern travel. But nothing of importance has really been affected. Human nature is still the same, and God does not change.

In fact, there is an advantage to old books. The things *we* take for granted may not be the same things they took for granted. The system adopts different tenets in different eras. We are shocked to find that our 'normal' view is condemned by the great teacher. It makes us stop and consider whether we could be wrong.

5. *We need patience and humility*

Of course, even with all the helps we can still end up with unanswered questions. We have to admit that we simply don't know. Why does God permit this?

Remember God's plan: we are to be made Christ-like. This includes knowledge, but it also includes humility. Finding out the answers increases our knowledge. But realising that we don't know shows us our weakness.

If we accept what God shows us of our weakness, then we acquire humility. Humility is essential, but sadly it is out of fashion. If I could see myself as I really am, beside God as he really is, I would see myself as virtually non-existent. He is great beyond our wildest dreams. It is to the degree I realise this that I am humble. If I am not humble, then I am not approaching God at all – not in reality, anyway. 'God resists the proud, but gives grace to the humble' (James 4:6). The proud can't get to God. The 'God' they think they know is mere fantasy. So a failure to understand the Bible may do us an unexpected good as we trust God and do our best, leaving the results to him.

Patience is another vital quality very much out of fashion. We live in an age of fast food and instant results. Computers give us information at extraordinary speeds. What used to take ages now takes a short time.

This is an age of miracles, for which we should thank God. A trip across the Atlantic takes mere hours compared with the danger-filled weeks of a couple of centuries ago. Even a few decades ago Mondays used to be 'washdays'. That meant that it took a housewife a full day to do the week's laundry. Now we are all familiar with washing-machines, tumble dryers and fabrics that don't need ironing.

However, all this is on the merely physical level. We cannot expect to learn about God any faster; we cannot expect him to sort us out any faster. Freedom from deception may come in an instant, as we saw earlier, but it takes a lifetime to gain a full understanding: 'Now we see in a mirror, dimly, but then face to face. Now I know in part, but then I shall know just as I also am known' (1 Corinthians 13:12).

So it makes no sense if I demand to have all my questions answered and all my ignorance removed *right now*. The underlying notion is that if we are now computerised and mechanised, surely God ought to be too! But put that way, we see a demand for instant results from God to be outrageous. In reality, patience is something we must learn. The only way to do so is to be kept waiting by God. If we can endure that without complaining, we have learned a great lesson.

LORD, my heart is not haughty,
Nor my eyes lofty.
Neither do I concern myself with great matters,
Nor with things too profound for me.
Surely I have calmed and quieted my soul,
Like a weaned child with his mother;
Like a weaned child is my soul within me.

(Psalms 131:1–2)

When a child is weaned, he has to learn to do without the comforting warmth of his mother's milk. This isn't easy, particularly if he is 'with his mother'. But why make the child suffer? Because the child has to get past this stage; he must be close to his mother without crying for milk. On the other side of the suffering is maturity.

It is the same on the spiritual level. We have to learn patience, to submit to the way God organises things, even though it is painful. We must be able to cling to God even though he is not giving us what we want.

Through this we learn not to be 'haughty'; we learn our limitations.

Expressing the Bible code

We have been using the word 'code' in the sense of a 'cipher' – something encoded. But 'code' has another meaning too. The Bible 'code' could be held to mean the standards and principles of the Bible.

This is a far cry from the sensationalism of the Bible Code. We are talking about the life – the code of conduct – that God reveals in the Bible. When people listen to God and learn from him, they begin to display that life in a visible fashion. People who wouldn't dream of opening a Bible – dupes of the system – see the 'code', the standards of the Bible before their very eyes in the Christian.

This is urgently needed. You and I are called to do it.

When this happens it makes a deep impression. You see, everyone knows deep down that love and kindness are what is needed. If everyone lied and stole, what sort of a society would there be? But as much as we know these things are needed, we need an incentive to be honest and kind. When the temptation comes, merely to say, 'But if everyone does this, society would be destroyed,' is not enough to restrain us.

Where do we get such an incentive? The threat of disgrace and prison may deter us from crime, but what stops us from being selfish? All the 'oughts' and 'musts' add up to nothing compelling, and our determined resolutions melt away in the face of strong temptation. It is very different with the Bible. Here is another mark of the Bible's unique potency. The Bible *does* give us a reason to be genuinely loving. On the one hand, there is the threat of endless hell. And then in the gospel there is a life-changing power, which makes the most selfish become self-denying.

Not so long ago there was a terrible crime committed by school children, and the British nation reeled with shock. Soon after, the government called for 'Christian' standards of behaviour to be taught in schools, but by 'Christian' they did not mean the love of God. They wanted children to be taught to be kind and unselfish.

I remember feeling so sad about the crime, and just as sad about the government's response. How can a school lesson really 'make' a child unselfish? How could anyone be so naive as to think it would? Sadly, people don't think straight when it comes to God. No, we must have a reason to love our neighbour – a motivation that really works.

This is where you and I come in. The Bible Code has caused a temporary sensation, a talking point for relaxed conversation. It might be good for one or two more bestsellers, and then it will be gone.

But the need for people to live out the Bible code of

conduct is constant. Will *you* study the Bible the way God requires? Will *you* live out what you find written there?

This brings us to the final chapter and the most exciting secret of them all: true transformation.

8
The Ultimate Secret

Books, codes, secrets and revelations; it's all very stimulating, but it's not enough. If that were all, we would discuss the matter with great interest, and then forget about it in daily life. We would mutter dark thoughts about conspiracies and the system, and then go on with our lives, completely unchanged.

If we stop here, all is for nothing.

What is the point of seeing that common sense shows us the true God if we live our lives independent of him? What if rationality points us to the Bible as God's book, and then we don't read it? Or worse still, what if we do read it, but remain unchanged?

Is all this just about adding to our knowledge? Are we merely feeding data into our brains? If so, we might as well have stayed with the Bible Code. Nothing else that has been said matters if we are not transformed.

You might call transformation the ultimate secret because although the church has proclaimed it for the last 2,000 years with varying degrees of clarity, few people seem to know about it. It is the primary message of the Bible. Are we in the know?

Commitment

Most people know that a person decides to become a

Christian, but they don't realise what a decision that is.
They think it is like any other choice; something that you
decide because you want to, and because you can.

Any of us *could* decide to join any of the groups and
clubs in our town – if they would have us! We would have
to make whatever commitments are required for member-
ship. For some, we would have to adopt new views. This is
easier than most people think. In practice, people are seen
to change their beliefs very smoothly. Love will lead people
to believe what the one they love believes. Not that people
are superficial and insincere, but we *can* change our beliefs
when we want to.

All these decisions, commitments and beliefs operate on
the human level. The transformation I am talking about is
above all of that. It is a supernatural event, and cannot be
duplicated by human resources. Did you know that?

We saw in Chapter 5 how this transformation is brought
about by 'the exceeding greatness of His power toward us
who believe, according to the working of His mighty power
which He worked in Christ when He raised Him from the
dead and seated Him at His right hand in the heavenly
places' (Ephesians 1:19–20). Anything less than that is not
the true transformation. The system prefers we forget the
whole matter, but if we must think about it, it has its own
man-made transformations with which to deceive us. Some
people think that belonging to a Christian family is
sufficient; others make church-going the same as being
transformed. For others, it is enough that they have chosen
to be a Christian, and still others make a 'good' lifestyle
their transformation.

All these things are good in themselves, but they all fall
short of the real thing.

When Jesus was visited by a religious leader, and before
the theological discussion could begin, he said: 'You must
be born again' (John 3:7). The phrase 'born again' is well

known, but do we know the reality behind it? If we have missed that, then no amount of good things will make up for it.

> Not everyone who says to Me, 'Lord, Lord,' shall enter the kingdom of heaven, but he who does the will of My Father in heaven. Many will say to Me in that day, 'Lord, Lord, have we not prophesied in Your name, cast out demons in Your name, and done many wonders in Your name?' And then I will declare to them, 'I never knew you; depart from Me, you who practice lawlessness!' (Matthew 7:21–23).

The point here is that on the last day people will be convinced that they are true Christians, but they will find out too late that they were mistaken. We learn that they will have claimed Jesus as their 'Lord', and will have been active – even highly successful – in his service. And yet all the way through their 'Christian' lives they were quite wrong: 'I never knew you,' Jesus says. How can people be so wrong? However we explain it, it is certain that 'many' on that last day will be appalled at their disastrous blunder.

It is madness to assume that we have the transformation without taking the trouble to be sure about it.

The true transformation

The Bible does not expect perfection in a Christian! 'If we say that we have no sin, we deceive ourselves, and the truth is not in us. If we confess our sins, He is faithful and just to forgive us our sins and to cleanse us from all unrighteousness. If we say that we have not sinned, we make Him a liar, and His word is not in us' (1 John 1:8–10). Those who are painfully aware of their sins and weaknesses need not feel themselves ruled out. The Bible reveals God in such purity and greatness that the very best people have felt themselves utterly filthy before him.

When the prophet Isaiah saw the Lord, he was dumbfounded. Although a holy man (as all the true prophets were) he cried out:

> 'Woe is me, for I am undone! Because I am a man of unclean lips, and I dwell in the midst of a people of unclean lips; for my eyes have seen the King, the LORD of hosts.' Then one of the seraphim flew to me, having in his hand a live coal which he had taken with the tongs from the altar. And he touched my mouth with it, and said: 'Behold, this has touched your lips; your iniquity is taken away, and your sin purged' (Isaiah 6:5–7).

Does that mean that Christians are no different from anyone else as far as lifestyle is concerned? Certainly not. In fact the easiest way to check whether you have been changed by God is to look at your life: 'Whoever has been born of God does not sin, for His seed remains in him; and he cannot sin, because he has been born of God' (1 John 3:9). This doesn't mean that the born-again person is perfect, as we have already seen. But it means there has been a transformation; instead of sin, his priority is to please God. This is more than a mere improvement: 'Therefore, if anyone is in Christ, he is a new creation; old things have passed away; behold, all things have become new' (2 Corinthians 5:17). This is no vague and general matter. God expresses it in terms of specifics:

> But the cowardly, unbelieving, abominable, murderers, sexually immoral, sorcerers, idolaters, and all liars shall have their part in the lake which burns with fire and brimstone, which is the second death [that is, hell] (Revelation 21:8).

> Now the works of the flesh are evident, which are: adultery, fornication, uncleanness, lewdness, idolatry, sorcery, hatred, contentions, jealousies, outbursts of wrath, selfish ambitions,

dissensions, heresies, envy, murders, drunkenness, revelries, and the like; of which I tell you beforehand, just as I also told you in time past, that those who practice such things will not inherit the kingdom of God (Galatians 5:19–21).

Do you not know that the unrighteous will not inherit the kingdom of God? Do not be deceived. Neither fornicators, nor idolaters, nor adulterers, nor homosexuals, nor sodomites, nor thieves, nor covetous, nor drunkards, nor revilers, nor extortioners will inherit the kingdom of God (1 Corinthians 6:9–10).

It is one thing to commit a sin; it is another to make it part of my lifestyle. These lists don't refer to the isolated fall, but the regular pattern. After all, I am no Olympic runner, even though I do sometimes go for a run. I am no car mechanic, even though I occasionally lift the bonnet of my car.

Nor should these lists make anyone despair. It isn't what we *have* done, but what we are doing. Followers of Jesus are sometimes among the worst people ever – once. The last quotation continues as follows: 'And such were some of you. But you were washed, but you were sanctified, but you were justified in the name of the Lord Jesus and by the Spirit of our God' (1 Corinthians 6:11).

Repentance

The word 'repent' is familiar enough, but what does it mean? It is more than feeling sorry, or turning over a new leaf. The enormous change is like a resurrection, and therefore the repentance that precedes it is a death.

Repentance isn't something that someone does whenever they feel like it. It is a supernatural process, an effect of the Holy Spirit. Jesus is said 'to give repentance' (Acts 5:31). That's why we read that Esau 'was rejected, for he found no place for repentance, though he sought it diligently with tears' (Hebrews 12:17). He didn't want to repent for the right reasons, and couldn't for the wrong ones.

The situation then is that 'he who covers his sins will not prosper, but whoever confesses and forsakes them will have mercy' (Proverbs 28:13). How tempting it is to cover over one's sins! How easily excuses come to mind! Things *we* do aren't so bad – it's only other people's sins that appal us! When we read the Bible, is it our sins that are revealed, or those of society around us?

In repentance, we come face to face with who and what we are. We realise that we are inexcusable. God, we see, has no reason or obligation to forgive us, let alone love us. We know that we richly deserve the endless torture of hell.

Repentance, therefore, is a sad and bitter experience. Out of it comes a hatred of sin, not merely of its consequences. It is a process that takes varying amounts of time. Once it is complete, we are convinced that if we are to go to heaven, it will be by sheer grace.

Now there is a new determination to do what pleases God because we *want* to, because he is the one we love.

It is so unfashionable to repent, that it seems impossible that anyone would think of it unless they were reading the Bible. The system insists that we have a good self-image, and tells us that true repentance is too miserable to be healthy. The cure of guilt, the system says, is forgiving yourself.

Someone who has only his own standards to satisfy will never truly repent.

The new birth

After the death of repentance, where everything good we have in ourselves is renounced, comes the spiritual resurrection. In the gospel we hear Jesus inviting us to trust him.

By now we know that we cannot earn God's favour. But all that we could ever ask for, and more, is offered to us in Christ. Faith, like repentance, is 'the gift of God' (Ephesians 2:8), and he delights to give it. We hear that 'God so loved the world that He gave His only begotten Son, that whoever believes in Him should not perish but have everlasting life' (John 3:16), and faith rises in our hearts.

By faith we are united with Jesus Christ. What is ours becomes his, and this applies to our sin – all of it. He takes it, and pays for it on the cross. The full punishment for everything in us which falls short of God's perfection falls on Jesus.

Realising this, we come to love him.

What is his as the perfect man becomes ours too. His righteousness, so attractive and lovable to God, is given freely to us. His life is ours too, both the earthly suffering and the eternal joy. 'God does not give the Spirit by measure' to Jesus (John 3:34), and we too are given the Spirit, to transform us into Christ's pattern.

There is so much more that could be said! The transformation is too sublime to be summed up in just a few words. The transformed are the children of God, and nothing will ever be the same again.

How can we describe these children of God? Jesus characterised those to whom the kingdom of heaven belongs:

Blessed are the poor in spirit,
    For theirs is the kingdom of heaven.
Blessed are those who mourn,
    For they shall be comforted.
Blessed are the meek,
    For they shall inherit the earth.
Blessed are those who hunger and thirst for righteousness,
    For they shall be filled.
Blessed are the merciful,

> For they shall obtain mercy.
> Blessed are the pure in heart,
>   For they shall see God.
> Blessed are the peacemakers,
>   For they shall be called sons of God.
> Blessed are those who are persecuted for righteousness' sake,
>   For theirs is the kingdom of heaven.
>
> (Matthew 5:3–10)

So these are 'blessed' people. Christ's blessedness means more than mere happiness. It is, after all, possible to be happy through sheer ignorance. Christ gives a true, deep joy, even in the midst of suffering.

Alongside this deep blessedness there are sorrows too. Christians are aware of their spiritual poverty, and 'mourn' their sin. They are not proud and arrogant, but 'meek', full of a Christ-like humility. They know that they lack further degrees of righteousness, and long intensely for them. Since they themselves deserve nothing, they offer to others the same mercy they have received. And, in the midst of their imperfections, they are pure in their intentions (their 'heart'), and even in this life they 'see God' by faith.

They make peace between God and people by passing on the Bible message of the gospel as best they can. Although they do it out of love, they are not surprised if the response is rejection and even persecution.

The best is yet to come

Does it seem inglorious that true believers still mourn their sin, and hunger and thirst for righteousness? Would we prefer a more 'superman'-like picture? The Christian is like Christ on earth who, in spite of his joy, was still a 'Man of sorrows and acquainted with grief' (Isaiah 53:3).

But the few decades of this life are only the start. There is an eternity coming, the Bible tells us. The importance that attaches to the things around us pales in significance when we think of eternity. What does money or prestige matter in comparison with heaven and hell? How can we complain about suffering if it is fitting us for unimaginable happiness for ever? And why hold on to sin if it merely fits us for hell? How will we feel about the pleasures of sin if we have an eternity to regret them?

The sufferings and glories of life only make sense when we understand them in Bible terms. In our society we don't think much about death. We don't prepare for the next life. We don't like people to mention such things because we see them as 'morbid' (how can heaven be morbid?).

The Kantian 'scientist' believes that our consciousness ceases with physical death; the Kantian 'mystic' feels that we all go to some happy place. Neither wants to think too rationally about it; both reject all thought of hell. They avoid the fact of Jesus' resurrection, and certainly don't wish to know what he said about eternal punishment. They choose fantasy rather than repentance. They want us to do the same. We are crazy if we do.

The Bible Code makes its little trip into predictions and the future. It is concerned about political events and the kind of things that are reported in the media. We have seen how contradictory the predictions are, but even if they were genuine, what do they really matter? Surely the future that really counts is our eternal future. Even the end of the world, from which Mr Drosnin thinks he has saved us using the Bible Code, is not as important as where we go after death. How sad that our society is absorbed by such earthly matters, to the complete neglect of the eternal.

Bearers of secret knowledge

Sensation follows sensation; the Bible Code will be followed by something else equally electrifying. Initiates will be full of the latest revelation, the new mystery, the next secret knowledge.

Meanwhile, they pass church buildings and meet Christians, and never guess that the real secret of life is hidden from them. No codes, or hidden tombs, or ancient hieroglyphics are as important as knowing the Creator of the universe.

But a true Christian knows God: 'This is eternal life, that they may know You, the only true God, and Jesus Christ whom You have sent' (John 17:3). This is not a secret that should be kept. Somehow or other, Christians must be more persuasive than the system. We must get past society's brainwashing, and let people in on the secret.

Happily, we have a secret weapon. God is at work, opening people's minds and sweeping the darkness away. He doesn't *need* our help, but he chooses to involve us in the process anyway.

There are two things we can do that are extremely powerful through God.

The first is to pray. We are called to pray for people. Since repentance and faith are God's gift, we cannot hope for any success unless God is at work. The Bible is full of wonderful promises that God will answer our prayers, so we can pray with confidence.

The other thing is to declare the truth, preach the gospel. With God, the gospel 'is the power of God to salvation for everyone who believes' (Romans 1:16). It really is powerful, and God uses it to break through the toughest prejudice.

All this is illustrated in a story Jesus told. He said that there was a beggar called Lazarus, and a rich man. When both died, Lazarus went to heaven, but the rich man was tormented in hell. There he saw matters in a very different light. He longed for his family to be warned, since they too were living as he had. He asked that Lazarus be raised from the dead and sent to warn them: 'If one goes to them from the dead, they will repent' (Luke 16:30).

Certainly we would have thought that people's prejudices are not so great that they would ignore the raising of a dead man! But alas that is the case. Some time later Jesus *did* raise someone called Lazarus from the dead. But did all those who knew of the event believe? Some, we are told (John 11:46), informed the Pharisees. They recognised that Jesus 'works many signs' (v. 47) – and then planned to kill him! Had they learned nothing from this raising of Lazarus? Apparently not.

This is what the rich man in hell was told: 'If they do not hear Moses and the prophets, neither will they be persuaded though one rise from the dead' (Luke 16:31). 'Moses and the prophets' means the Old Testament; the Bible so far as it had then been written. If people won't listen to the Bible, even amazing miracles won't break through to them.

Nowadays they would probably attribute it all to UFOs!

So it's up to us to pass on the Bible message. It isn't intended to be a secret. Don't be timid! The message of the gospel is amazingly powerful. It can achieve more than the appearance of someone raised from the dead. Don't despair that the system keeps the truth off the bestseller list! God is able to change all of that when the time is right.

The Bible is *the* bestseller, after all!

Appendix

The Hebrew Language

During the course of this book the reader may have acquired an unenthusiastic view of the Hebrew language. The strangeness of the letters alienates most people, and now they hear that the vowels are mere dots and can easily be omitted, with disastrous results.

And what about Hebrew tenses? We saw in Chapter 2 that Hebrew verbs are rather complex: could it really be that 'the future is always written in the past tense, and the past is always written in the future tense' (*The Bible Code*, p. 175)? If this is truly the situation with Hebrew, why did the Holy Spirit use it in the writing of the Old Testament?

This little appendix is designed to vindicate Hebrew from these wrong impressions and, if at all possible, to sow in the reader the beginnings of a desire to learn the language. 'What, learn Hebrew?!' But why not? Why not hear the *actual* words of God? Learning Hebrew is not as difficult as it sounds.

But first, the vindication.

Why the dots?

Written Hebrew requires more effort than written English. Observing the exact position of each dot is harder than merely skimming the letters on a page of English.

119

But is easiness everything? Being a Christian is not 'easy', but it is glorious. There is a glory in the Hebrew language which is not to be found in English. Let us see some of what that is.

There are twenty-two different vowel sounds in Hebrew. This isn't just complexity for its own sake. The vowels in a word can shorten and grow softer in its different forms. This happens in English too: we slur some of our vowels. For instance, the 'e' in 'the' is impossible to write in English: we don't say 'e' as in 'them', but something that sounds more like 'uh'.

In Hebrew, all this is reflected in the actual vowels. This means that, unlike English, the Hebrew spelling tells you how the word is pronounced. There is even a dot (':') for our unpronounceable 'uh' sound! I find this very reassuring. It means that I savour the actual words of God, because their spelling tells me how they sound. This would not be possible if the vowels were not dots. Even if twenty-two new letters could be found, they wouldn't do the same job. There is a dot that looks like a '+', but without the top stroke. When it becomes weaker, it loses the bottom stroke and looks like '–'. You can actually *see* it weakening. How would you do that with letters?

And then each word has a dot to tell you where to put the emphasis. In English, you can't distinguish between 'entrance' (the way in) and 'entrance' (to captivate). It all depends on where you put the emphasis when you say it. In Hebrew, this sort of ambiguity cannot occur. The emphasis dot tells you what you need to know.

But the emphasis dot does more than that. It tells you how the word fits into the sentence. It tells you whether the word belongs with the last word, or the next. It is a highly sophisticated form of punctuation. It even tells you how closely a word is attached to another word. There are twenty different dots to show you how closely a word belongs to the one before it!

By contrast, our punctuation is far more sparse. We have only five signs (- . : ; ,) to give us the rhythm of a sentence. If you use these signs too much, it is bad style. Just imagine how much you could convey with the Hebrew system! No wonder God used it!

The student of Hebrew may not have been taught much about the punctuation. The standard twentieth-century Hebrew grammar, Kautzsch's *Gesenius' Hebrew Grammar* (OUP, 1910), ignores it. The older version of *Gesenius' Hebrew Grammar* by E. Roediger (Albert Cohn, 1876), gives a helpful account, saying that it shows 'the logical relation of each word to the whole sentence' (p. 48).

When you read the Hebrew, you get a superb feel for the rhythm and sense of the sentence. There is so much in God's words! Are you still sure that you don't want to learn this wonderful language?

What about the tenses?

In English we have past, present and future tenses. We want to know whether a thing *has* happened, *is* happening, or *will* happen. It is all very precise and factual. You can get this from the Hebrew too, but its main interest is somewhere else. The verbs tell you whether a thing is finished or not.

The two basic Hebrew tenses can be called 'past' and 'future' for the English student, but it would be more interesting to say 'finished' and 'unfinished'. Usually, a 'finished' action is in the past, so why not just call it the 'past' tense?

The answer is, because God is timeless. Very often, when he is predicting what he will do (our future tense), he uses the Hebrew 'finished' tense. This doesn't mean that the predicted thing is already past – that would be ridiculous –

but that it is as good as done in God's mind. 'It is done,' says the Lord in the book of Revelation (21:6) about things still future.

The point is, we are getting a sense of God's attitude, his determination. What he promises will infallibly take place. It is impossible to translate this into English. These tenses take a bit of getting used to at first, but once you get the hang of them, you realise that you get more from a Hebrew verb than you can from the English.

And you still don't want to learn Hebrew?

You can get something of the splendour of the actual words of God in Greek and Hebrew from *The Newberry Bible*.[1] In it the Authorised Version of the Bible is printed with a system of signs and symbols to represent some of the untranslatable riches of the original.

When John Newton, the author of 'Amazing grace', was converted in the eighteenth century, he immediately gave up being a slave-trader. He had virtually no education, but he set out to learn Hebrew and Greek. He lived in revival days, very different from ours, so perhaps we shouldn't expect to see such eagerness today.

But then again, why not? He knew nothing that we don't also know. He simply put it into practice. 'If the Bible is God's book,' he thought, 'then I want to know it as well as I possibly can.'

Perhaps, when we follow the Lord with that degree of determination, it will be revival days again.

---

[1] My copy is a reprint by the Penfold Book and Bible House, 1987.